AFRICA AND THE RISE OF CAPITALISM

By Wilson E. Williams

AND

NEGRO DISFRANCHISEMENT IN VIRGINIA

By Robert E. Martin

AMS PRESS

NEW YORK

Vol. I

No. I

The
HOWARD UNIVERSITY STUDIES
in the
SOCIAL SCIENCES

AFRICA AND THE RISE OF CAPITALISM
By Wilson E. Williams

AND

NEGRO DISFRANCHISEMENT IN VIRGINIA
By Robert E. Martin

Howard University
Washington, D. C.
1938

Library of Congress Cataloging in Publication Data

Williams, Wilson Elbe.
    Africa and the rise of capitalism.

    The authors' theses (M.A.)—Howard University.
    Reprint of two works issued in 1938 by Howard
University, Washington, in v. 1, no. 1 of Howard
University studies in the social sciences.
    Includes bibliographical references.
    1. Great Britain—Commerce—Africa. 2. Africa
—Commerce—Great Britain. 3. Slave-trade.
4. Negroes—Virginia—Politics and suffrage.
I. Martin, Robert E. Negro disfranchisement in
Virginia. 1975. II. Title.
HF3508.A3W55   382'.0942'06   79-144702
ISBN 0-404-06987-8

From the edition of 1938, Washington, D.C.
First AMS edition published in 1975
Manufactured in the United States of America

AMS PRESS INC.
NEW YORK, N.Y. 10003

HOWARD UNIVERSITY

THE DIVISION OF THE SOCIAL SCIENCES

Board of Editors

Chairman

Abram L. Harris

Associates

Alain L. Locke   Charles H. Wesley   Emmett E. Dorsey   W. O. Brown

Members of the Division

Ralph Bunche, Professor of Political Science; Walter Dyson, Professor of History; E. Franklin Frazier, Professor of Sociology; Abram L. Harris, Professor of Economics; Julius E. Lips, Visiting Professor of Anthropology; Alain L. Locke, Professor of Philosophy; Charles H. Wesley, Professor of History; W. O. Brown, Assistant Professor of Sociology; Edwin E. Lewis, Assistant Professor of Economics; Jesse W. Lewis, Assistant Professor of Commerce and Finance: William B. West, Assistant Professor of Commerce; Emmett E. Dorsey, Instructor of Political Science; H. Naylor Fitzhugh, Instructor of Commerce and Finance; Eugene C. Holmes, Instructor of Philosophy; J. Walter Fisher, Instructor of History; Ruth Jackson, Instructor of Social Work; Harold O. Lewis, Instructor of History; Hylan Lewis, Instructor of Sociology; Inabelle Burns Lindsay, Instructor of Social Work; Williston H. Lofton, Instructor of History; William P. Robinson, Assistant in Political Science; and John Syphax, Assistant in Political Science.

CONTENTS

1. Foreword

2. Africa and the Rise of Capitalism.....Wilson E. Williams

3. Negro Disfranchisement in Virginia......Robert E. Martin

Foreword

Only within the past decade has any serious attempt been made at Howard University to develop and expand those disciplines which are generally grouped as the social sciences. That this is true of an institution which has been advertised and accepted as the "Capstone of Negro Education" will no doubt appear strange to one who is unacquainted with the history of Howard University, in particular, and the Negro problem, in general. This failure of the University is partly attributable to a kind of unconscious division of labor that gradually took hold of the Negro colleges after their establishment in the wake of the Civil War. Fisk, Atlanta, Virginia Union, Talladega and other colleges and so-called universities were to furnish Negroes with a liberal education and thus to feed the professions and the graduate schools of the great American universities. Howard came to be looked upon as the center of professional education in which medicine and dentistry assumed predominance.

Although the offerings in liberal arts were more varied at Howard than at any other Negro college, the role of medicine at Howard tended to stimulate the natural sciences and thereby to stunt the social sciences. Faced with the necessity of building a strong Medical School, it was inevitable that the University should place greater emphasis upon the natural sciences than upon the social sciences and make greater provision for the former. It is no accident then that on the whole the most significant research and the best instruction in the natural sciences in Negro institutions of higher learning has been conducted at Howard. In this connection one needs only to mention the internationally famous work of Professor Just in the field of cytology. But while medicine has caused the natural sciences to be more greatly emphasized and provided for than the social sciences, its importance in the curriculum has not been without serious drawbacks upon the natural sciences themselves. If the best students gravitated to Chemistry, Physics, and Biology, as most of them did up to ten years ago, they remained in these subjects only long enough to fulfill the basic requirements for entrance into the Medical School. The development of pure research and scholarship has under the circumstances had rough sledding.

It was but natural, given the economic exigencies of the race problem, that most of the best students could only conceive of the natural sciences in terms of equipping themselves for the Medical School. Shunted away from business and commerce and without inherited wealth, the Negro saw in the professions of medicine, dentistry, and to a lesser degree, law, his only opportunity of realizing the great American dream of escaping poverty into riches. These professions, especially medicine, promised lucrative careers and social prestige in the segregated Negro community. Years of training and research in the natural sciences would lead to no such financial rewards or social esteem. The Negro trained in the natural sciences could look forward to the teaching profession as his one source of possible employment. What was true of the natural sciences in these respects was even truer of the social sciences. But there were other factors responsible for the backwardness of the social sciences at Howard University.

In the past "Social Science" in the conception of the chief executives of Negro institutions of higher learning and the philanthropists who financed them was but a euphemism for "Negro problem". Situated midway between the North and the South and devoted primarily to professional education, Howard University was thought to be too far removed from the black belt to feel the impact of the race problem. It was "out of touch" with the predominantly agrarian Negro population and was therefore "unreliable" as a guide in the amelioration of Negro problems. It was thought that the southern colleges and such industrial schools as Hampton and Tuskegee were better fitted by temperament and location to deal with Negro problems and to suggest remedies for them. However, with the exception of Atlanta University, and perhaps Fisk, not one of these colleges or industrial schools developed even second rate courses in Economics, Government, Anthropology, and Sociology. Only at Atlanta University was significantly scholarly work begun in the social sciences. In the 90's under the direction of Dr. W. E. B. DuBois the Atlanta University Studies made their appearance. But DuBois' monumental beginning was cut short by inadequate financial support. At Fisk the work of the sociologist, Dr. George E. Haynes, was shortlived but his early study of the Negro migrant in New York led to the founding of the League on Urban Conditions of Negroes in New York, which subsequently became the National Urban League. In the other Negro colleges, the teaching of the social sciences was either confined to the most elementary principles or banned altogether as dangerously radical.

In criticising the development of the social sciences at Howard University, one should not overlook the early contributions of the Departments of History and Commerce and Finance. In 1914 and 1915, two studies on banking and business were made by Professor George Hines of the Department of Commerce and Finance. In 1921, the Howard University Studies in History were begun. These Studies stamp the two departments as pioneers in social science research at Howard. In addition to the work of these two departments that of isolated individuals at the University should be mentioned.

Leaving mathematics for sociology in 1919, Professor Kelly Miller, now retired, came to be celebrated as one of the leading sociologists of the Negro race. In 1905, he published "As to the Leopard Spots", a polemic against Thomas Dixon. Two years later his "Race Adjustment" appeared. Keen of wit, a gifted

satirist and controversialist, Professor Miller was essentially a race leader
and a pamphleteer who steered a middle course between the Washington and DuBois
schools of racial advancement.

The publication of the "History of Negro Labor in the United States"
by Dr. Charles H. Wesley in 1927, marks the beginning of authentic social
science research at Howard. This was followed by a local study, "The Housing
of Negroes in Washington", by Professor William Jones in 1929. Although
technically not a social scientist, Alain Leroy Locke, Professor of Philosophy,
as the editor of "The New Negro" (1925) and the sponsor of a number of other
works, has provoked scientific interest in the race problem both inside and
outside the University.

Since 1926, Howard University has undergone a remarkable expansion in
personnel and physical plant and equipment. The social sciences shared in this
expansion but not as fully as some of us had hoped and expected. Only ten years
ago the request for an adding machine for use in the social sciences provoked
amusement. Today, a statistical laboratory equipped with several adding
machines and calculators is accepted as necessary scientific equipment. This
is something of an indication of the great change in the status of the social
sciences in the University in the past decade. But much more indicative of the
change is the awakened interest of students in the study of economic and social
problems. This has been brought about partly by the pressure of outside
economic conditions and partly by the work of the younger men who joined the
faculty within the last ten years. Much remains to be done before the social
sciences can begin to function on a satisfactory basis. The pressing need is
adequately financed graduate fellowships and research. While it is true that
persons who subsidize research and fellowships in Negro colleges are still inclined to look upon Howard as a center primarily of professional education, the

excellence of a university must be achieved not simply in medicine, dentistry, law, and teaching, but also in the broad phases of human knowledge.

In carrying forward work in the social sciences at a Negro institution, it is to be expected that the study of the economic and social problems of Negroes should engage a large part of our time and energy. If the future is to be judged by past publications of members of the faculty, one can rest assured that these problems will not be neglected. We feel that in studying the problems of Negroes, the investigator must begin with the proposition that these problems are an integral part of American life. If, for example, we study the Negro farmer and share-cropper, or the Negro business man, we must study them not as isolated phenomena but in connection with general changes in agriculture and business characteristic of the American economy as a whole. Furthermore, we do not believe that the study of Negro questions should engage our attention to the exclusion of problems of a more general nature. Some of us, by our publications, have already demonstrated interest in these problems. And it is hoped that in the future more will do so.

The Negro scholars of this generation in the social sciences, if we at Howard can be taken as typical of them, are unlike their predecessors. They do not consider themselves race leaders or social reformers. They are interested in the quest of knowledge for the sake of knowledge. They believe, nevertheless, that research which is disinterested in means and ends, and which is content with the accumulation of facts, is sterile. The social scientist, in the words of Alfred Marshall, must be "greedy of facts". But he should know that facts without interpretation do not speak for themselves. Fact gathering is only one step in scientific investigation. As a scientist the student of social problems is under obligation to generalize his factual findings into a body of systematic conclusions.

It is believed in some circles that we at Howard are more inclined to abstraction and "theorizing" than to the arduous task of factual research. In view of some of our publications it is incredible that such an opinion should persist among the informed. Purely factual, or what has frequently been dignified in the Negro colleges as statistical research, may be just as biased as so-called theoretical studies. The old methodenstreit in the social sciences lies buried, we hope, in the intellectual graveyard of the nineteenth century. We shall be the last to ressurect it. For, in our opinion, all methods, the historical, the statistical, and the abstract have their peculiar advantages and disadvantages. It must be left to the investigator to decide which method best suits his particular problem. But whatever method is used, research must always be guided by "trained common sense". In brief, we believe that teaching and research in the social sciences require both technical competence and point of view.

In inaugurating the Howard University Studies in the Social Sciences, the Division hopes to create a permanent channel for presenting to the public the best contributions of graduate students and some of those of the faculty. In the present volume we present two essays, "Africa and the Rise of Capitalism" by Wilson E. Williams, and "Negro Disfranchisement in Virginia" by Robert E. Martin, submitted for the Master of Arts degree in Economics and in Government in the school year, 1937-38. The Studies in the Social Sciences supplant the earlier Studies in History. Our desire is that this new series will appear regularly and, hereafter, in printed form under the impress of the Division of the Social Sciences, Howard University.

Abram L. Harris

AFRICA AND THE RISE OF CAPITALISM

By Wilson E. Williams

* * * *   * * * *

CHAPTER I

Max Weber, Werner Sombart, Richard Ehrenberg, R. H. Tawney, and others have all dealt with the problem of the evolution of capitalism. No one, however, has sought exhaustively to ascertain the relationship of Africa to the problem. In several places in his works, Karl Marx makes significant observations on the relation of African gold, slave labor, and the slave traffic to the development of European commerce and industry in the 16th, 17th and 18th centuries. But Marx's comments are incidental to his main argument. The purpose of this essay is to make a beginning in the study of this important but neglected topic.

One of the conditions for the development of capitalism is a landless working class. By virtue of the agricultural changes in Europe, nearly all of the western European powers possessed a working class which by the eighteenth century was bereft of the ownership of land and the tools of production. Most of these "propertyless workers" became wage laborers in the evolving industrial system. Some of them migrated to the New World where eventually they became independent farmers and planters. The colonial economy which thus arose in the New World became connected with the expanding commerce and industry of western Europe not simply by the fact that it supplied the European industry with raw materials such as tobacco, indigo, sugar, and cotton, but also by the fact that the survival of the colonial economy depended upon a constant flow of slave labor supplied by European traders. In brief, the traffic in slaves helped to swell the overseas trade of expanding European capitalism and the exploitation of the slave on the colonial plantations supplied England, the "Mother of Capitalism", with raw materials for her expanding industries.

Expanding markets and production from 1500 to 1800 made metallic money more necessary than ever as a means of business accounting, a common denominator of exchange, and a store of value. Under Spanish and Portugese exploitation, the Americas furnished large supplies of gold and silver in the late 16th and 17th centuries. Later Africa was forced by English merchants to yield considerable quantities of the yellow metal. In addition, then to expanding markets, there were three necessary conditions for the development of capitalism: (1) a surplus of labor population which was without productive property; (2) an adequate supply of metallic coin; and, (3) the existence of a class of daring men, resourceful, and willing to assume the great economic risks in the hope of gain. The Dark Continent furnished some of the first and second. Europe supplied the last of these.

It was in England that modern capitalism first began. England possessed peculiar advantages for the evolution of the capitalist economy. Isolated from the European mainland she was able for the greater part to remain relatively aloof from the devastating wars that played havoc with the economy of continental countries from 1400 to 1700. Furthermore, her excellent harbors, homogeneous population, and paternalistic governments were also important factors in her early supremacy in the overseas trade and her leadership in colonization.[1] The numerous pamphleteers of the seventeenth century, even the poets, as Cowper, were enthusiastic in their support of trade activities. One writer, William Loddington,[2] set forth the case for colonization with the sound argument that thus might the poor find freedom and work. Earlier, Richard Eburne[3] had concluded that plantations were "a certaine necessitie", as they would support "the king's regall estate which take much from his subjects" and rid the country of excess population, which "like stalls that are overfull of bees, or orchyards overgrowne with younge sets, no small number of which should be transplanted into some other soils".[4] The same author wrote that "the benefit that might that way accrew unto merchants, and all kinde of adventurers by sea, is infinite".

To the leading mercantilist writers overseas commerce was the sensible course of action. Malachy Postelthwayte, one of the later mercantilist writers, wrote: "It is agreed on all hands that the mere inland trade of the nation cannot sustain the maritime prowess.....What can more effectively prevent the fatal catastrophe than the support of our foreign trade?"[5]

It was this sort of England, then, to which mercantilist writers addressed their words, encouraging manufactures but extolling the great benefits of overseas trade. Colonies were regarded as the means of national wealth and power. This idea of acquiring riches appealed to the rulers who were ever on the alert for new sources of revenue made necessitous by their lavish courts. The English kings were unstinting in their aid.[6] Queen Elizabeth, first of the English rulers clearly to appreciate the worth of the African trade and, to profit therefrom, was most liberal in granting patents to merchants who sought to secure trade relations with the African dealers.[7]

Mercantilist philosophy[8] pervaded English economic thought virtually without opposition until Adam Smith's time. Gustav Schmoller defines this philosophy as "a policy of economic unity to overcome internal disruption".[9] And, Heckscher states[10] that the English people of the period, believing that consumption was of no value in itself, "came by easy strides to the notion that only an excess of income over expenditure increased the riches of a country".

The England that was dominated by mercantilist thought was in need
of raw materials for her manufactures, and of the labor power necessary for
her colonial empire-in need, in brief, of the requisites for the erection of
a capitalist economy. The English government, in keeping with popular opinion, was of the proper mind to foster the trade. By the beginning of the
eighteenth century conditions were such as to render the trade with Africa
of paramount importance to the nascent capitalist economy.[11] It is with this
period that this essay is primarily concerned. English markets, commerce and
industry began to undergo a terrific expansion by the first of the seventeenth
century; and a study of this period reveals the extent to which the trade to
Africa was necessary to the development of capitalism in England. Our investigation is confined to the English trade with Africa, the slave trade, and
the trade between England and her colonies in the West Indies. No attempt
has been made to study the North American colonies which require separate
treatment.

CHAPTER II

Trade to Africa was begun, says Bryan Edwards,[1] by a Portuguese, Anthony Gonzalez, who carried some Moor prisoners to Africa. In exchange for the prisoners Gonzalez received ten blacks and some gold dust which he carried home to Lisbon. This incident led to the establishment of a Portuguese fort on the Gold Coast in 1481.

In 1502 the Spaniards, having found the native Indian labor unsuited for employment in the mines of Hispaniola, began importing Negro slaves. In 1517 Charles V granted a patent to certain merchants who sold it to Genoese merchants. This patent gave the Genoese merchants the privilege of supplying Jamaica, Cuba and Puerto Rico with 4,000 slaves annually.[2]

The English, however, did not take an interest in the trade to Africa until about 1536, when certain traders made a voyage to Guinea.[3] Hakluyt states that one James Aldaie claimed to have originated the trade to Barbary.[4] Captain John Hawkins, the first Englishman to participate in the trade on a considerable scale, left England in October, 1562 for Sierra Leone. Here he "took by sword and otherwise" 300 Negroes, carried them to Hispaniola and traded them to the Spanish colonists. He returned to England with great profit.[5] So profitable, indeed, was the voyage that the Queen, Elizabeth, and the Earl of Leicester sponsored his second voyage, the Queen furnishing one of the three ships used.[6] Hawkins set out for a third time in 1567. This time he was compelled to deposit a bond of 50 pounds against trading with the Spanish colonies. Thus encouraged, a regular traffic was built up by 1564. The failure of Hawkin's third voyage, however, delayed further English expeditions.[7] But in 1588, Elizabeth granted patents to a group of Exeter and London merchants for pursuing trade in Senega and Gambria in Guinea.[8] On the whole, England's trade with Africa was at this time, of slight significance. Although an essentially agricultural country, England by conquering the Spanish Armada had laid the basis for her future commercial supremacy.[9] And it was not until 1641 that the need for slave labor was greatly augmented by the introduction of sugar cane from Brazil into the English colony of Barbadoes.[10] During the reigns of James I and Charles I, England was engaged primarily in supplying Spain with goods. These goods Spaid had hitherto purchased from Holland, with whom she was now at war.[11] But, in 1654 Cromwell broke the peace with Spain, and for a period the English lost this trade.

English trade in slaves reached significant proportions only after the Assiento was granted in 1713. The great profits were derived from this trade only with the turn of the seventeenth century. A pamphlet published in 1659[12] made the claim that "100 sail of ships" were employed in this trade, but this was not found to be substantiated by any other author. The West India Company, formed for the purpose of acquiring lands in the West, had taken a fort from the Portugese on the Gold Coast;[13] but the Dutch West India Company claimed the sole right to certain lands along the Gold Coast and accordingly intercepted all other traders. To strengthen the English traders, the King united them into the "Company of Royal Adventurers Trading Unto Africa, January 10, 1662.[14]

In 1672 the Royal African Company was formed to supercede the "Company of Royal Adventurers"[15] The importance of this new company in preserving the trade to the English was described by an early mercantilist author, Charles Davenant. Davenant showed that although the company was usually in debt, many of its members amassed great profits through mis-application of funds or by sheer fraud.[16] The Duke of York was the company's first governor, and later King William himself took over the governor ship.[17] According to Postlethwayte, Sir Jonathan Andrews of East India fame, Thomas Pindar, leading London merchant, Sir William Withers, merchant and member of parliament and formerly Lord Mayor of London, all were members of the company. Over the period 168-1688, Postlethwayte gives English exports to Africa as averaging over 70,000 pounds sterling per annum.[18] Previous to the organization of the Royal African Company, private traders had sought to override the monopoly enjoyed by the "Company of Royal Adventurers". In America, the colonists of Virginia and Maryland petitioned the House of Commons, December 7, 1669, complaining that the company seized all the ships and effects of the separate traders who formerly had supplied the colonies with blacks, "and would not send so much as one slave thither themselves".[19] This seizure of ships resulted after Parliament had opened the trade to all interested persons, in 1667, and imposed a tax of 10% on all goods exported to Africa. This tax afforded revenue to defray the expenses of the company, but in addition the company found it necessary to spend over 30,000 pounds of its annual income. The character of this early trade to Africa was described by Postlethwayte. That author wrote[20] that England sent to Africa brass, amber, blankets, bells, beads, cloth, carpets, pistols, gunpowder, silk, hats, knives, beef, bread, butter, sugar, medicines and liquors.[21] From Africa in return for these English goods came gold, camwood, beeswax, elephants' teeth and dyewoods. According to the same author, "It is to be remembered that these goods were sold to a great advance, about one hundred percent."[22] Custom House certificates showed, Postlethwayte continued, that 1153 pieces of woolen manufactures were made especially for the African market during the years 1657, 1658, 1660 and 1661; that 500 persons were given employment in the manufacture of annabasses, nicanese, etc. designed for African consumption and that 100 persons at Kidderminster were engaged in the striped carpet manufacturies and other establishments dealing in goods for African trade.[23] The trade from 1663 to 1686 amounted to 103,644 pieces, or one hundred times more than when it was first opened.[24]

In 1710, its stock exhausted, the Royal African Company petitioned Queen Anne. The Queen hastened to send out men and provisions to preserve the forts. By 1712, the company owed 298,000 pounds. This indebtedness was met by issuing stock to the creditors who were compelled by executive order to accept this means of payment. Between 1720 and 1723 the company raised 524,000 pounds in this manner and "fell a-trading and a-digging through the mountains in search for gold".[25] All this was done because the company was considered so necessary for the African trade. It was impossible, Postlethwayte argued,[26] for private traders to reap the full benefits of the trade, as the Dutch and French seized all boats. Thus, it was only through the maintenance of forts that the English could hope to retain anything like an equable share of the trade.

The trade to Africa was hampered not only by European rivals but also by the precariousness of the trade itself. The African natives gave the European traders no little worry; for example, in 1678 the agent of the Company advised the home office against the construction of forts, as they were in constant danger of appropriation by the African Kings. One of these kings, Amoniah, caboceer of Cape Appolonia, the "richest man in all Guinea", was "a great spirit for trade".[27] The Gold Coast Fantees "would laugh in a man's face if told that by some English act of Parliament they have the right of trading with whomever they choose, for it is a liberty they have constantly taken, as the undoubted right of a free people; so free that, upon the slightest disgusts, they have often made free with the chiefs themselves".[28] This author felt that the chiefs should be given the right to trade directly with the West Indies. The home office advised the agents to "treat the natives gently"; and the 23d act of George II imposed a fine of 100 pounds for any violence to them.

It was in the slave traffic that the African chiefs exhibited their power of shrewd bargaining. Postlethwayte complained that some of them charged unduly exorbitant prices for their slaves.[29] The trade in blacks was looked on by the African chiefs as their main source of income. The development of large parts of Africa had been held back by numerous causes, not the least among which was the presence of the tsetse fly which was so detrimental to cattle and beasts of burden. Hence, it was natural that the African traders were pleased to offer as their chief article of export a commodity that would walk to the market, namely slaves.[30] The chiefs were almost incessantly at war with each other. Rivalry between tribes was provoked by European traders who would assist the chief most inclined to grant them a monopoly on his slave market.

As mentioned above, English concern with the African trade assumed serious proportions mainly insofar as this market became an apex in that triangular trade which developed after the colonies.[31] But, for the purposes of this paper it may be worthwhile to consider the African market itself. Some of the Africans, it seems, were not always of strict honesty. The owners of the brigantine "Two Brothers" of Liverpool instructed the ship's chief officer to "take a deal of care they do not cheat you and see it be sifted clean. The dust is more valuable, but they are grown so cunning that they cut the fatish gold in small grains and mix it amongst the dust which lowers the price very much. Gold dust is worth four pounds sterling per ounce, and the fatist[32] is not worth above three pounds five shillings."[33]

It was the traffic in slaves, however, that served to stimulate English manufactures, at the same time constituting a source of tremendous profits. As stated above this trade attained significant proportions in the early part of the eighteenth century, when Bristol and Liverpool rose as the great centers of the trade.

The Portuguese first found use for the African slave in their Brazilian colony and the Spanish people followed closely behind their neighbors. As already noted, it was not until the turn of the century that England came to a full realization of the importance of the trade. She was concerned with Africa primarily as a source of gold and as an outlet for her nascent manufactures. The trade was very important even aside from the traffic in slaves, as many pamphleteers argued. One of the writers of the period asked, "Are the exports to the coast of Africa and imports from thence, considered even abstractedly from the negroe-trade and the preservation of our colonies in America, of no consideration to Britain?"[34] John Cabess, King of Commenda, possessed a most unique relation with English traders. King John was the "most powerful negro on the Gold Coast, having a large quantity of gold dust and near 300 men fit to bear arms, mostly his own slaves".[35] Having quarreled with the Dutch traders, Cabess sought English aid and agreed to contribute to the expenses of the erecting of an English fort at Commenda. One author used this incident to fortify his argument for the support of the Royal African Company. He said that the forts are "to be situated as to support them who support our trade"[36] This trade to Africa, as distinct from the later triangular commerce, consisted generally of the goods which Africa could absorb in exchange for its gold, ivory, wax and dyewoods. In Postlethwayte's words the English goods thus traded were comparatively insignificant when compared with the later trade which brought the West Indies into the circuit. It became possible, under the triangular arrangement, to dispose of practically all surplus goods, there being almost no limit to the number of slaves offered for trade. This satisfied the principles of the mercantilist theorists who desired never to export money, although even gold was sometimes sent to Africa after the slave trade reached its peak. When the slave trade reached important proportions, the Gold Coast became a leading market for English manufactures. In fact, as will be later shown, English exports to Africa frequently exceeded all other branches of that country's export trade.[37] During its best days Whydah's king sold to the English about 20,000 slaves per year, taking English manufactures in exchange.[38] And the population of the African west coast was so dense that one writer averred that exportation of Africans could not harm the remaining blacks by causing any noticeable diminution in population.[39] Thus, in one sense, it was left entirely to Europeans to determine the extent to which this market was to be exploited.

At this time England's main industry was cotton and woolen manufacture. Although England shipped goods of different kinds to the African market, its chief export was cotton and woolen cloth. As the African natives were very fond of colorful materials it was usually an easy matter to dispose of a cargo.

Bristol became an important center for the trade in slaves about 1700 and enjoyed undisputed leadership until Liverpool began to challenge it in 1709. According to one author, the London and Bristol merchants enjoyed greater wealth than those of Liverpool, and thus secured an early start on the Liverpool traders. Bristol merchants sent an average of 57

ships per year to the dark continent between 1701 and 1709,[40] of which the
approximate value was 377,231 pounds sterling.[41] A Bristol merchant, John
Cary, said that the trade to Africa was "a trade of the most advantage to
this kingdom of any we drive, and as it were all profit; the first cost
being little more than small matters of our own manufactures, for which we
have in return, teeth, gold, wax and negroes, the last whereof is much better
than the first, being indeed the best traffic the kingdom hath as it doth
occasionally give so vast an employment to our people both by sea and land."[42]
These Bristol merchants maintained that the prosperity of the West Indies
was dependent on a regular supply of Negroes, and that consequently their
wares must continue to be sold in Africa.[43] It was only after Bristol
became interested in the African trade that her shipbuilding absorbed so
much labor[44] and began to afford profitable opportunities for investment of
capital in manufactures. Thus, Bristol's growth as an important shipping
center was, as one writer put it, "peculiarly dependent on her place in that
triangular trade on which the commercial supremacy of all England rests".

William Miller, grocer and banker, was one of the chief Bristol
merchants who acquired their fortunes in the Africa-West Indies-England triangular trade. By 1785 Miller's fortune was estimated to exceed 190,000
pounds sterling.[45] Other large fortunes were acquired by John Bricdale and
Zachary Bayley whose holdings amounted to 100,000 pounds each. John Andrews
with 90,000 pounds; David Peloquin, merchant and sheriff in 1736 and mayor
in 1751, with 80,000; Joseph Percival, Henry Hobhouse (master of the Society
of Merchant Adventurers in 1788), Michael Atkins, Jeremiah Ames, and the
drapers firm of Gough and Burgess all built up fortunes estimated at 70,000
pounds each. William Miller, the above mentioned Bristol merchant, is known
to have advanced loans to merchants of Bristol as well as to plantation-owners.

Many Bristol merchants had seen service in the West Indies, and so were competent dealers in the African slave trade. For example, one Harrington Gibbs returned home from his station in the West Indies to become the agent for Beckford, Dawkins and other West India planters. Being acquainted with the tastes of the Africans, Gibbs was able to prepare cargoes for the Gold Coast with goods more likely to please the natives.[46] Still more concerned with the triangular trade was Robert Cann, mayor of Bristol in 1662 and again in 1675. Cann had large holdings in the West Indies, was a leading merchant and used his own ships for transporting goods.[47]

But neither Bristol nor London ever reaped the vast profits from the trade in slaves that Liverpool amassed. Not only did Liverpool become the principle English export market for goods sent to Africa, but her more enterprising merchants made the city an important slave market. Once the merchants of Liverpool entered the field the ascendancy of the merchants of Bristol and London began to give way. In the early part of the eithteenth century, the merchants of Liverpool began to export provisions, coarse checks and silk handkerchiefs to the West Indies and to the northern colonies. These early shipmasters were beseeched by the western planters to "bring a few slaves on the next trip". Thus Liverpool was stimulated to participate in the lucrative traffic in blacks.[48] Her participation began with the fitting out of "The Blessing" in 1700, for the Gold Coast, Whydah and Angola. The slaves obtained were to be sold in the West Indies and the return cargo was to consist of sugars, ginger, cotton and indigo.[49] Liverpool cargoes were frequently created on the basis of credit purchases from Manchester manufacturers. In some cases the goods were supplied by warehouses maintained at Liverpool by the enterprising Manchesterites. The overseas commerce of Liverpool was originally a creation of relatively small capital which grew steadily into

large fortunes. For example, a brigantine sent from Liverpool in 1717 had
five owners, three of whom had quarter-shares each while two had one-eighth
shares. A merchant who died in 1711 left quarter-shares valued at about 60
pounds sterling in three ships and a sixteenth share in another valued at
50 pounds.[50] A ship sold in 1732 realized 492 pounds which was distributed
among four owners. Between 1717 and 1725 another merchant who engaged in
the trade had shares in seven different ships. A 90-ton brigantine, a priv-
ateer in the African trade was owned in 1744 by six merchants.[51] It would
seem, then, that the amount of capital invested and accumulated was small in
the first half of the eighteenth century. By 1725 Liverpool was engaged
extensively in the African trade. The number of ships employed had increased
from one or two in 1700 to about twenty three. At this time London had 87
and Bristol 63 ships engaged in the African trade. In this year exports to
Africa totaled 218,704 pounds sterling, of which some 66,000 pounds worth
were of English home manufacture. The latter figure is in sharp contrast to
the value of goods shipped to the African Coast in 1701. In 1701, the value
of English manufactures exported to Africa was 13,954 pounds. Thus, in a
period of twenty five years the value of goods exported by English manufacturers had significantly declined. This was caused by a change in African
taste. The Negroes had begun to demand larger varieties of goods.

In 1752, Liverpool had almost caught up with London and Bristol.
In that year the ships putting out for Africa from that city numbered 101,
while those from London numbered 135 and from Bristol 157. The relative de-
clines were great for both the latter cities.[52] The value of the goods
shipped to Africa in that year was 236,026 pounds sterling of which 147,012
pounds worth was of English manufacture.[53] In 1750 by an act of Parliament
George II established a company "for extending and improving the trade to

Africa belonging to Liverpool". By virtue of their influence in the company
the Liverpool merchants were able to have most of the goods of Manchester
shipped through Liverpool. In 1764 ships for the African coast carried more
than a quarter of the shipping of Liverpool, and Liverpool merchants conducted more than half of the country's trade with Africa.[54] In this year the
value of goods sent to Africa was 464,878 pounds, about 324,800 pounds being
of English manufacture. Thus, the share of Liverpool must have been at least
233,000 pounds sterling. Of cotton piece goods, the amount going to Africa
increased more than that going to the West Indies in the period from 1759 to
1769, when Liverpool achieved ascendancy in this trade. This increase,
largely in checks, fustians and prints, amounted to about 150% for goods
going to Africa and to about 25% for goods for the West Indies.[55]

In 1714 the "Wakefield Gallery", owned by four Liverpool merchants,
was built for service in the African trade. The owners, however, were lacking in courage and were fearful of the risks involved in the business of
dealing in slaves. They agreed to let the ship out to whomever would stock
her for the voyage. The chief officer, who it seems had already acquired
some experience in the African trade, arranged with two Manchester manufacturers, John Dyson and Thomas Touchet, and one Mathew Wilson of Worthy Forge
to put on a cargo of dry goods worth 300 pounds. This, with other small
consignments, brought the total to 800 pounds. The cargo included ticks and
fustians of which the Touchets were to become leading manufacturers in the
1750's. Cotton and sugar were returned from the West Indies, and the trip
netted a profit of about 100 pounds sterling per owner.[56] Again, the owners
of "The Two Brothers" instructed their chief officer in 1717:

> "We shall leave it to you to touch at what place you think
> most proper at first to wood and water, only would have
> you keep enough to windward as far as Gamboe, and then no

doubt but you will have room enough to trade from thence
to Cape Three Points, there will be no buying of slaves
beyond, they will be so dear, be sure you do not overrun
your market but try all places and endeavor to purchase
healthful slaves if you give dearer for them.....We would
have you take up what gold and teeth you can as you trade
along and some Malageta pepper if you can purchase it
cheap. Whenever you depart the Coast make the best of
your way to Antigua, and when you arrive, try the market
and if you can sell slaves for bills of exchange take
freight for London, Bristol or this port, but buy no sugar on our account,[57] but what cotton and ginger you can.

"But in case the market does not answer there you may pro-
ceed with your slaves to Nevis, St.Xfer or Mountserrat,
and in case you do not find encouragement there and the
slaves continue healthful, we would have you go down to
Jamaica, which we look upon to be the likest market and
there dispose of them for ginger, cotton and indigo and
weighty dollars and take freight. Notwithstanding what is
said above, if you find sugars so low as they will now
serve the markets as they are we leave it to you to purchase what quantity you please".[58]

Some months earlier the same owners instructed the officer of an-

other of their ships:

"If you find the finest sugars are cheapest considering the
goodness of them, would have you purchase such but we think
that indigo and ginger are more to our advantage than sugar
..... Cotton is very low and like to continue. Here are several accounts from Jamaica that negroes are in great demand
there. If you should meet with such poor markets at Barbadoes that they will not bring 20 pounds per head running
would have you stop at any place on Jamaica".[59]

Again, the "Ann" was fitted out at a cost of 1,219 pounds and em-

barked for the Coast with a cargo valued at 385 pounds. The slaves secured

were sold to merchants at Antigua. Bills of exchange were brought home val-

ued at 2,006 pounds, while the sailors' wages were 138 pounds, leaving 1,767

pounds to be divided among the six partners. Later, the Antigua merchants

remitted the balance due, 1,519 pounds. Thus, this voyage netted 3,287

pounds.[60]

Mr. Thomas Leyland, Liverpool banker, owned the "Lottery". In 1788 his share from the sale of 453 Negroes was more than 20,000 pounds. In 1802, the same ship carried 305 Negroes to Jamaica, the voyage netting 19,021 pounds plus a few hundreds more made on the rum and sugar brought back.[61] Profits were the rule on these trading trips, although the traffic was a particularly hazardous one. By 1795, the bulk of the trade was in the hands of ten large shipping houses.[62] A list of the owners of the slave ships operating out of Liverpool includes almost all the leading merchants of that city. These ships with their capacity is as follows:[63]

Ships	Owners	Capacity (in slaves)
Africa	John Welsh Company	250
African	J. Manesty	250
Annabella	W. Dobb and Company	260
Antigua Merchant	James Gildart	200
Angelsey	Tine, Farrar & Company	180
Alice Galley	R. Cheshyre Company	350
Ann Galley	William Whalley & Co.	340
Adlington	J. Manesty	320
Allen	J. Brooks and Company	250
Achilles	Henry Hardware Company	450
Betty	John Robinson	100
Blake	Jo. Bird and Company	460
Barbadoes	G. Campbell & Company	500
Boyne	E. Forbes and Company	400
Beverley	E. Lowndes and Company	200
Brooke	Roger Brooks Company	400
Barclay	John Welsh Company	450
Bulkeley	Foster Cunliffe[64]	350
Britannia	Thomas Leatherbarrow Co.	300
Bridget	Foster Cunliffe	250
Clayton	Foster Cunliffe	250
Cumberland	E. Deane and Company	260
Chesterfield	W. Whalley Company	440
Charming Nancy	W. Davenport and Company	170
Cavendish	Nicholas and Company	170
Cecelia	Fr. Green and Company	120
Duke of Cumberland	T. Crosbie and Company	450
Dolphin	Ed. Forbes Company	200
Elizabeth	Sam. Shaw and Company	200
Elijah	E. Lowndes Company	200

Ships	Owners	Capacity (in slaves)
Enterprise	John Yates	130
Ellis and Robert	F. Cunliffe	320
Eaton	John Okill	550
	(Dealer in wood and teeth)	
Fanny	J. Knight	120
Ferret	John Welch	50
Florimel	Richard Townsend	320
Frodsham	Nich. Torr and Company	480
Fortune	Henry Townsend	480
Foster	Foster Cunliffe	200
George	G. Campbell Company	250
Grace	Ed. Forbes and Company	400
Greyhound	Rd. Savage Company	120
Hesketh	R. Nicholas Company	260
Hector	W. Gregson Company	480
Hardman	J. Hardman	300
Jenny	John Knight	450
Judith	John Welch	350
James	James Gildart	400
Knight	R. Nicholas	400
Sterling Castle	John Backhouse	300
Samuel and Nanax	R. Savage	220
Sammy and Biddy	J. Blundell	120
Schemer	T. Chalmers	120
Stronge	M. & J. Stronge	300
Lintott	R. Nicholas Company	400
Lord Strange	William Halliday	230
Lovely Betty	George Campbell Company	140
Little Billy	J. Knight Company	60
Mersey	J. Kennison	300
Middleham	R. Gildart	280
Methwen	T. Grosbie	280
Minerva	James Pardoe	400
Mercury	Kennison & Holme	100
Molly	R. Golding	320
Neptune	J. & J. Brooks	450
Nelly	William Williamson	320
Nancy	T. Kendall	400
Nancy	Peter Holmes	400
Nancy	Knight, Mairs Company	300
Orrel	W. Whalley	120
Ormond Success	William Williamson	300
Paradoe	James Pardoe	240
Priscilla	John Welch	350

Ships	Owners	Capacity (in slaves)
Phoebe	A. & Ben. Heywood	280
Prince William	R. Gildart	200
Rider	R. Gildart	300
Ranger	W. Farrington	300
Sarah	T. Crowder	550
Salisbury	Robert Armitage	350
Swan	John Tarleton	400
Tarlton	John Tarlton	340
Triton	Levinus, Unsworth	240
Thomas	G. Campbell	200
True Blue	J. Cheshyre	300
Thomas and Martha	G. Campbell	300
Vigilant	J. Bridge	160
Union	J. Pardoe	350
William & Betty	S. Shave	400

The "Company of Merchants Trading to Africa", founded as remarked above by George III, was composed, in 1750, of the following persons (it will be noted that a good many of these merchants appear on the preceding list of slave-ship owners):[64]

John Bridge Aspinall
James Aspinall
William Aspinall
Daniel Backhouse
John Backhouse

John Barnes
Ralph Benson
Robert Bent
Patrick Black
Jonas Bold

John Bolton (Boulton)
P. W. Brancker
Joseph Brooks
John Brown
George Brown, of Wales

James Carruthers
George Case
Henry Clark
Thomas Clarke
Samuel Clough

William Harper
B. A. Heywood
Thomas Hinde
Thomas Hodgson
James Hodgson

H. B. Holinshead
Francis Ingram
John Chambres
Peter Kenion
John Langton

Roger Leigh
George Lewis
William Neilson
Thomas Parke
Thomas John Parke
Thomas Parr
Thomas Parr, Jr.
James Penny
Jonathan Radcliff
William Riggs
John Sanders

Edgar Corrie	Christopher Shaw
William Crosbie	Bryan Shaw
James T. Cukit	George Spencer
John Dawson	Samuel Staniforth
Edward Dickson	Thomas Tarleton
James Dickson	Thomas M. Tate
William Dickson	William Thompson
Thomas Earle	James Watt Kinson
William Earle	Richard Willis
William Forbes	William Watson
James Gregson	Richard Wilding
James Gildart	William Woodville, Havana
Thomas Golightly	Planter
John Greenwood	Richard Woodward
William Harding	

The growth of Liverpool to a trade center of world importance may be taken as generally indicative of the evolution of the capitalist economy in England. At first glance it might seem that Liverpool owed its growth to its nearness to the manufacturing district known as the Lancaster section. It is the purpose of this essay to show that exactly the reverse was true: that is, Liverpool made the manufacturing district, thus illustrating more concretely the importance of Africa in the evolution of capitalism.

Before the seventeenth century Liverpool was hardly more than a mere village. But the sheltering estuary of its harbor was already attracting trade.[65] In 1709 the natural harbor was widened, and the trade to Africa got under way with the fervor already mentioned. As late as 1770 the factory system had hardly begun around Lancashire,[66] and although Manchester was an active and prosperous town, its cotton products were as yet of relatively poor quality and quite incapable of competing with East Indian goods.[67] It has already been mentioned how the Manchester manufacturers had set up warehouses in Liverpool, in order to have wares ready for shipment to Africa. So many African traders bought goods on credit, in order to get into the very lucrative slave trade that this building of warehouses was but natural. For example, the Hibberts had estates in Jamaica, and were Manchester check-makers: checkmakers before dealers in slaves, it is true; but the impetus given their business by the presence in the West Indies of one of the Hibbert sons, to whom many Liverpool merchants consigned their shipments of slaves, cannot be overestimated. In the 1760's this firm supplied the African Company with most of their checks and imitations of Indian goods.[68]

Then there were the Touchets. Thomas Touchet (1678-1744) began exporting ticks and fustians in 1714.[69] He left a fortune of nearly 20,000 pounds besides large annuities to relatives at Warrington. Samuel Touchet, his son, was the London representative of the firm and he subscribed 420,000 of the eight million pound government loan floated in 1759.[70] His shipping interests included insurance brokerage, speculations in prizes and extensive bill dealings. In 1751 the same Samuel Touchet was negotiating with Lewis Paul concerning Paul's invention, a roller-spinning machine. Touchet was considering financing Paul, but the deal seems not to have been completed.[71]

Such men as the Touchets and the Hibberts, and the Banker Leyland made Manchester possible through their trade activities. The existence of waterpower in the Manchester neighborhood was indeed favorable to the development of the factory system, but this was a common situation in England; and other similar endeavors to erect a factory system were not followed with the success attendant on the Manchester growth.[72] Each factory represented a capital of several thousand pounds, and it has been shown how Liverpool's vast business in slaves was shared among the Manchester manufacturers, if in no other way even than the purchasing of goods for the African trade. According to Aiken,[73] Manchester was the trade center for the area of about 15 miles around, using much labor in its production of calicoes, fustians and brightly colored piece goods which found so ready a market in the African native villages. Liverpool was in close contact with the African and the West Indian markets, so that Manchester manufacturers found here a ready market for their wares. For example, the house of J. & N. Philips & Company, founded in 1744 at Manchester, was engaged in every branch of the Manchester trade: silk, fustians, checks, West India merchanting, cotton spinning and power-loom weaving.[74] Again, Sir William Fazacherly, a director of the Royal African Company and a London dealer in cloths, purchased most of his own stock from the Manchester makers, as well as negotiating for a large amount of the goods for that company's trade to Africa. In 1750, for example, Mr. Fazackerly ordered of the Manchester firm of Newdigate and Ford "as much cotton as you can afford at 12 d. per yard", and almost all the Company's purchases of loincloths appear to have been made through Mr. Fazackerly who got them from the Manchester houses at considerably less cost than he sold them to the Company.[75]

The growth of Liverpool was too closely parallelled by the extension of the trade with Africa to permit of any doubt as to the source of its prosperity. It is common knowledge that the slave trade afforded to British shipping its most lucrative source of revenue; and we have seen how Liverpool stood at the lead in this traffic. Since Liverpool made Manchester, the connection of Africa with the evolution of capitalism in England is thus rendered very clear.[76] When the trade was at its highest point, in the last decades of the seventeenth century, the average return on voyages in the triangular trade was estimated at 30% and Liverpool was said to have a clear gain of 260,000 pounds sterling per year as her share of the traffic.[77] Between 1783 and 1793 Williams states, 359 firms sent 878 cargoes to Guinea, 502 of these cargoes being sent by ten large houses.[78] According to Privy Council reports, this decade witnessed a traffic in African slaves averaging 74,000 per year. The various European nations interested in this transporting of blacks to the western colonies shared the trade as follows: Great Britain, 38,000 per year; France, 20,000; Portugal, 10,000; and Holland, 4,000. Of the 814,000 slaves carried to the West Indies in those ten years, it is estimated that Liverpool "had the profit and disgrace of conveying 304,737".[79]

The slave traffic, however unpleasant to present-day morals, was one of the greatest sources of profit in the early development of English capitalism. Doubtless much of this activity was profitless, but even apart from the profits derived from the traffic in slaves, Africa was of paramount importance as an outlet for the English surplus products, as well as a source of gold for coinage. And, the persons employed in the pursuit of the trade must have been of no small number. Of English exports to Africa over the century 1680 to 1780, those of domestic manufacture amounted to 11,881,443 pounds sterling.[80] This figure does not include exports between 1689 and 1700 for which estimates are lacking. Sir William Petty states that in 1690 a total of more than 20,000 slaves were transported to the plantations.[81] At the rate of three and a half pounds each,[82] the gross receipts were at least 50,000 pounds which should be added to the above figure. It is probably not extreme to assume that a century of trade with Africa in goods of English make approximated 15,000,000 pounds sterling. The exports of cotton goods alone for that period were valued at 167,635 pounds.[83] The total English exports to Africa for the period was at least 50% in excess of the figure estimated for home manufactures. These statistics support the thesis that Africa was a "most important" outlet for English manufactures and that it was directly responsible for the increasing number of persons employed in turning out such products. Furthermore, the growth in the concentration of capital, a notable characteristic of modern capitalism, is illustrated in this connection by the fact that by 1795 most of the business was in the hands of ten large shipping houses. A large part of the profits from this trade was invested in England's vast textile industry. The growth of English shipbuilding and merchant marine is likewise to be attributed to this trade.

In order to reveal more clearly the importance of Africa in the evolution of English capitalism it will be worthwhile to examine in detail some of the efforts to exploit that continent's articles that entered this branch of English commerce. The search for gold, the necessary basis for the monetary system which capitalism required, cannot be treated exhaustively. Full statistics on the importation of the yellow metal are not available. Even before England had embarked on overseas expansion, the dark continent had been brought into the orbit of the germinal stage of capital accumulation. The early English traders had long been engaged in supplying Africa with whatever goods she would take, bringing home gold, ivory, beeswax and certain woods. It is to the writings of Richard Hakluyt that we must turn for details on this early trade with the Gold Coast. In 1555, says that author, one William Towrson, a London merchant, sent out two ships, the Hart and the Hind, with John Ralph and William Carter as captains. These ships carried to Africa cloths-basons, manellios and margants and brought back various grains, gold and teeth.[84] The captain made the following comment on this voyage:

> "We tooke some of every sort of our merchandize with us, and
> shewed it to the negroes, but they esteemed it not, but made
> light of it, and also of the basons which yesterday they did
> not buy; howbeit for the basons they would have given us
> some graines, but to no purpose, so that this day we tooke

not--one hundred pound waight of graines, by meanes of their captain, who would not suffer no man to sell anything but through his hands, and at his price; he was so subtile, that for a bason hee would not give 15 pound waight of graines, and sometimes would offer us small dishfuls".[85]

On another day on this same voyage, the ships took in 7 pounds, 5 ounces of gold, and a third day some 25 ounces.[86]

A second shipment was sent out by the same Towrson, the vessels being the Tiger of London and the Hart. The trading on this trip was as follows:[87]

"1 day -- half Angel weight of gold and 4 grains

1 day -- 1 ounce, for which he gave 80 manellios

1 day -- 30 ducats of gold taken in trade

1 day -- 5 pounds, seven and a half ounces gold

1 day -- 4 pounds, 6 ounces

1 day -- 5½ ounces gold

1 day -- 8¼ ounces gold

1 day -- 5 pounds, 1¾ ounces gold

1 day -- 19 pounds, 3½ ounces gold

1 day -- 2 pounds, 6½ ounces gold

1 day -- 3 pounds

1 day -- 1 pound, 5 ounces gold

1 day -- 5 pounds, 6½ ounces gold

1 day --   4 ounces gold

1 day -- 1 pound, 2½ ounces gold

1 day -- 5 pound, 1 ounce gold

1 day -- 1 pound, 4 ounces gold

1 day -- 4 pounds, 1 ounce gold

1 day --   3½ ounces gold

1 day -- 1 pound, 10 ounces gold

1 day -- 3 pounds, 7 ounces gold

Thus, although Towrson was forced to trade on the coast for a
month, gold was so important an item that he decided to send out even a
third convoy.[88]

This time the ships were the Minion Admiral, the Christopher
Viceadmiral and the Tyger. On the first day of trading 2¼ ounces gold and
19 elephants' teeth were taken. Seizing a French ship which had been trading in the neighborhood, Towrson's convoy returned to London bearing gold
in excess of 65 pounds in weight and a load of ivory. Other ships engaged
in this early trade to Barbary were as follows: Thomas Stuckeley who made
a voyage in 1578.[89] Robert Cainshes whose trip to Guinea in 1554 resulted
in the capturing of the African captain's sons and all his gold;[90] the Lion
of London of which Thomas Windam was captain, set sail for Morocco in 1551,
carrying as cargo linen, woolen cloth, coral, amber, jet, etc;[91] in 1553
the Primrose, the Lion and the Moone, with sevenscore men brought home 150
pounds of gold;[92] in 1554, the Trinitie, the Bartholomew, and the John
Evangelist, brought home 400 pounds gold, 250 elephant's teeth and 36
butts of grain;[93] the Richard of Arundell, owned by Bird and Newton, London
merchants, carried beads, bracelets, cloth and iron and brought back teeth,
palm-oil and cloth made from bark on its first voyage[94] but on its voyage
in 1590 the ship carried out kersies, broadcloth, linen, iron, hats, bracelets, etc., and returned with gold as well as the other staple articles.[95]
The trip made by Richard Rainolds and Thomas Dassel of London, in the
Nightingale and the Messinger also resulted in gold.[96] The Royal African
Company was instrumental in augmenting England's gold supply in the later
years. So important was the Guinea cost in supplying this metal that as

an encouragement to the company the king issued a warrant that the master
and worker of the mint were to coin all gold and silver brought there for
the use of the African company into guineas as a distinction from the other
English coins.[97]

CHAPTER III

**** _____ ****

The tie-up between English capitalist development and the colonial empire should be examined more closely. Ties between the colonies and the mother country were both political and economic. Our interest is in the economic. While Eburne and Loddington were convinced of the importance of colonization, Adam Smith was a bit skeptical. Smith wrote,[1] for example, "The establishment of the European colonies in America and the West Indies arose from no necessity: and though the utility which has resulted from them has been very great, it is not altogether so clear and evident".[2] But Marx's opinion differed from Smith's. It was Marx who first emphasized the importance of slavery as a foundation of the capitalist order. He said: "Slavery is an economic category just as any other. Direct slavery is the pivot of bourgeois industry, just as are machinery and credit, etc. Without slavery there is no cotton; without cotton, there is no modern industry. It is slavery that has given value to universal commerce, and it is world trade which is the condition of large scale industry. Thus, slavery is an economic category of the first importance."[3] As we have noted it was around 1642 that the need for slaves was felt in Barbadoes, when sugar cane was introduced from Brazil. A prominent feature in the African and West Indian trades was the "certain assurance that the only capable cultivators were negroes".[4] Native Indians were highly intractable and died very rapidly when subjected to exploitation in mines and on plantations. Beside, the Indian population was not nearly large enough to supply the plantations with adequate labor. Thus, it was early recognized that another source of labor had to be found.

Africa came to be looked upon as a virtually inexhaustible source of labor.
Subsequently, the legend arose that only African Negroes are capable cultivators of sugar and cotton. The men who participated in the African slave
trade were interested only in deriving profit from the sale of their human
cargoes. But to the plantation owners the African slave was essential in the
exploitation of the new world.[5] William Beckford, a Jamaica planter and a
member of the English parliament said, "It has been contended that the population of our islands may be preserved without the introduction of foreign
slaves; and one or two properties have been quoted as a corroboration of
this fact: but what is the partial advantage of three or four, to the calcu-
lation of one-thousand-and-fifty one which are now settled in Jamaica alone?"[6]
Postlethwayte felt that "As negro labor hitherto has so that only can support our British colonies, as it has those of other nations".[7] According to
Edwards' account, "The arrival of a Guinea ship is announced by public adver-
tisement, specifying the number of negroes imported, the country from whence
and the day of sale." The sales were at first held on shipboard, but the
buyers became so aggressive and "began so disgraceful a scramble that the
poor Africans were terrified with the notion that they were set upon by a
herd of cannibals and were speedily to be devoured."[8] According to the same
author, the profit from the labor of each field Negro might be reckoned as
25 pounds sterling annually.[9] A sugar plantation was normally expected to
yield "as many hogsheads of sugar as there are negroes employed on it".

A description of the Island economy further exhibits the connection
between slavery in the colonies and the evolution of English capitalism. In
1643 there were 18,600 Englishmen in Barbadoes, 8,300 of whom were proprietors.
At this time the value of the island was not one-seventeenth of what it came
to be 1666. In 1666 the value of the plate, jewels and household goods on the

island was estimated as 500,000 pounds sterling. Writing in 1665 to the Sec-
retary Lord Arlington, John Stylus said he thought that Jamaica "exceeded
England in all things". He found the island so profitable that he would have
resolved to end his days there had he not been so deeply engaged at home.
But he sent for his two sons to bring grain, plows and tradesmen. Stylus
said that a man with 100 pounds could live here in greater plenty than one in
England with as much as 200 pounds per year, and in a few years the settler
could acquire a valuable estate.[10]

It was about this time that the African Company began to represent
that the trade to Africa was "so necessary to England that the very being of
the planters depends upon the supply of negro servants for their works".[11]
In 1662 the Company sent about 160,000 pounds worth of goods to Africa,
"plentifully supplying the coast, furnished the plantations with negroes,
set up new manufactures at home and improved the old, vented many native commodities, and doubt not to import much gold and silver".

By January 22, 1670 Jamaica products were employing yearly 20 ships
of 80 tons and were exchanging for about 18 shiploads of English goods.[12] In
that year the firm of Jacob Lucie, Samuel Synoke, John Bovey and Company sent
their ship the "Mary and Jane" to Africa with a cargo valued at 7,566 pounds,
the slaves purchased being sold at Jamaica. As evidence that Jamaica was
thus early a very important out post of the British Empire it is noteworthy
that in 1670 the island had 717 families and about 15,000 persons; 57 sugar
works, producing about 1,710,000 pounds of sugar per year, 47 cocoa walks
producing 186,000 pounds of nuts, 49 indigo works, as well as pepper, salt
and ginger enterprises.[13] Cromwell had already (1664) assured the settlement of Jamaica by granting 20 acres to each male 12 or over who would take
up land,[14] and many Englishmen hastened to put in claims. Most of the

claimants chose to remain at home, however, and **absenteeism** came to be the
normal form of proprietorship in Jamaica. The following is a list of such
landholders in 1670:

Owner	Acres
Thomas Amor	10
Southwell Atkins	1,070
Charles Barnett	90
John Bassett	78
Thomas Booth	12
William Basnett	60
Capt. Thomas Browne	1,060
Joseph Barger	11
Francis Butterfield	30
Samuel Backs	200
Christopher Cooper	690
Caesar Carter	60
Gawell Crouch	100
Thomas Carpenter	6
John Clarke	90
Josiah Child	1,330
John Davenport	340
Francis Davis	120
Thomas Evans	215
Stephen Evans	330
Col. Thomas Freeman	1,309
Capt. Hendrix Molesworth	2,480
William Mosely	1,242
Thomas Modyford	6,090
Lt. Col. Robert Freeman	1,338
Sir James Modyford	3,500
Major Richard Lloyd	1,370
Richard Richardson	1,034
Henry Archboule	2,030
Lt. Col. Richard Hope	1,497
James Howell	1,233
Capt. William Powell	1,534
Francis Scarlett	1,000
Thomas Tothill	1,300
Charles Whitfield	950
Capt. John Bourden	2,255
Lt. Col. Robert Bindlos	1,935

Owner	Acres
Capt. Thomas Ballard	2,391
Mr. More	1,000
Henry Hilliard	1,668
Capt. Joachim Hans	1,550
Capt. Samuel Long	2,200
Capt. Coleback	1,340
Maj. Antony Collier & Mates	2,600
George Elkins	3,286
Bartholomew Fant	1,130
Maj. Thomas Fuller	1,309
Richard Hemmings	1,600
John Halkins	1,190
Samuel Lewis	1,555
George Needham	1,764
Capt. John Noye	5,868
Jonathan Cook	1,000
Sir James Modyford	1,000
Capt. Robert Nelson	1,300
Capt. George Reid	1,403
John Styles	3,200
George Booth	1,200
Peter Beckford	2,235
Joseph Bathhurst	1,200
Maj. Anthony Collier	1,261
Lord Clarendon	3,000
Capt. Edward Collier	1,020
Capt. Christopher Horner	1,083
Lt. Col. William Joy	1,070

The evils of absenteeism, accentuated as time passed, are described by one writer as the fundamental cause of the 19th century collapse of the island empire.[16] Concerning absenteeism the complaint of Nicholas Blake against Richard Lewes, Richard Jones, Richard Rice, et al is interesting. Blake alleged that these men had "by subtlety goty the whole means of the poor laborers engaged to them, and yearly heap interest upon interest and gnaw them to the bone, and such exactors take 30 per 100 per annum and more. Some in England live rich upon it, and certainly Nehemiah is needed to deliver those poor men out of their bondage."[17] A source of absenteeism was the

desire of many persons to extract the greatest amount of wealth in the shortest possible time. Thus, in Jamaica, particularly, a man sought to make his
hoard as quickly as possible and return to England to live in ease and luxyry
on his oversea investment. As evidence of the prevalence of absenteeism in
Jamaica may be cited the fact that generally all the more lucrative offices
on that island were held by Englishmen residing at home. The governor with a
salary of 6,000 pounds per year almost invariably resided in the mother country, leaving his duties to be performed by a deputy. Similarly, the offices
of Provost Marshall, clerk of the Supreme Court, the Register in Chancery,
the Naval Officer and the Collector of Customs were all usually held by persons residing at home, their deputies remitting about 30,000 pounds annually
in payment for their jobs.[18]

At another time, 193 attornies, mortgagees, guardians, etc., were
holding (in lieu of debts owed them) 606 sugar works, and 3,987 tierces of
sugar, all valued at 4,022,460 pounds sterling.[19] It was said that "The
great planters will swallow up the small ones, and the middling planters will
dwindle in their turn."[20] Still another cause of absenteeism was the fact
that the wealthy planters sent their children to Europe to be educated, and
these generally chose to remain abroad.[21]

Barbadoes, however, was an island of small plantations, and the
concentration of ownership which characterized Jamaica was never known here.

Absentee ownership and the flow of capital from the islands to the
mother country are both illustrated in the controversy that the West Indian
trade robbed England of investment funds. One writer replying to the accusa-
tions of John Dutch[22] insisted that, "...wealth does flow to the mother
country. No such fund existed from the beginning: From the first commence-
ment, it grew with the growth of the colonies. A settler in the West Indies

accumulates a few thousand pounds, and desires to purchase an estate worth six times that amount and a mortgage is given to secure the balance."[23] The merchant advancing the loan usually did so on the basis of his past accumulations from the colonial and African trades. The same author argued also that young men migrated, and by degrees accumulated capital, much of which was sent home to support their estates there. Such merchants were by that very process enabled to make loans, and the effect was a cumulative one. Since the market for sugar was a peculiarly difficult one to gauge,[24] many of the planters were constantly in debt. Frequent mortgage foreclosures caused a great many plantations to fall into the hands of absentee owners. Thus, ownership was often transferred to persons who had never seen a plantation. In many instances the owners never once visited their island holdings, for example, William Miller, the Liverpool banker, whose loaning activities caused him to take a deep interest in the proceedings for remuneration of plantation slave-holders in the abolition fight.

According to Bryan Edwards,[25] the usual cotton plantation, 50 acres in size, involved an initial investment of 1,040 pounds sterling distributed as follows: 250 pounds for the land, 175 pounds for clearing, 840 pounds for 12 negroes, 195 pounds for one year's interest and maintenance of laborers. The returns from such a plantation, with an average yield of 112 pounds of cotton per acre, at an average price of 1 shilling 3 pence per pound, 25 cwt. of cotton should bring 175 pounds sterling. Deducting 25 pounds for incidental expenses, a "profit of 150 pounds is accrued, or about 14 per cent on the capital out-lay.

A coffee plantation of 300 acres involved an out-lay of 10,960 pounds. Adding interest at 6%, the initial out-lay may be taken as 13,053 pounds. Annual expenses on such a plantation were as follows: 200 pounds to white overseer, 70 pounds to one other white servant (usually a bookkeeper), 25 pounds for doctor's fee, 200 pounds for clothing for the negroes and 100 pounds for taxes. Coffee requiring about three years of profitless operation, Edwards estimated that in about five years the return from such a plantation should amount to about 24 1/2% on the yearly out-lay.[26]

For sugar cultivation the same author estimated the cost of a 600 acre plantation as 30,000 pounds sterling allocated as follows: land, 10,071 pounds; buildings, 5,000 pounds; 250 Negroes, steers and mules, 14,557 pounds. The annual produce on such a plantation Edwards reckoned to be 200 hogsheads of sugar which, at 15 pounds each, would bring 3,000 pounds, and 160 puncheons of rum which would net 1,300 pounds. Thus, the total annual return would amount to 4,300 pounds. Deducting 1,300 pounds for freightage, salaries, etc. this author concluded that a return of about 2,100 pounds or 7% would be derived. The same author estimated that the return on an English farm of about the same size would not yield more than 4%.[27]

Thus, the islands were an important field for investment of English capital. The merchants of London, Liverpool, Bristol and Glasgow made heavy advancements to the planters, many of whom, as stated above were not at all capable managers. The 5th of George II and the 13th and 14th of George III were acts passed expressly for encouraging loans to plantation-owners. In 1790, loans outstanding to West Indian planters totaled more than 70 million pounds sterling.[28]

Postlethwayte estimated the annual import of sugar, indigo, cotton, etc., from the islands at a value of about 1,300,000 pounds, one-third of which was usually reexported.[29] In 1728 an anonymous author contended that Jamaica alone was employing 300 ships requiring 5,000 sailors which he held, were in readiness for naval service.[30] In 1740 John Ashley pointed out that rice imports from the islands amounted to 50,000 barrels per year and were valued at 80,000 pounds sterling. This, Ashley argued, afforded employment to ten thousand tons of shipping and 900 sailors.[31] As early as 1676, the produce of Barbadoes shipped to Britain was valued at 350,000 pounds per year.[32] It was estimated that in 1787 there were 143 water-mills costing 715,000 pounds; 20,000 hand-mills costing 285,000 pounds; and 350,000 persons employed in manufactures, all contingent on the production of and traffic in West Indian goods.[33] The value of the total imports from the islands in the eighteenth century exceeded 209,000,000 pounds sterling.[34]

As an outlet for English manufactures the West Indies were very important. In 1734 the Commission for Trade and Plantations represented to the House of Lords that the annual exports to the island colonies were worth 880,000 pounds.[35] The plantations were generally well stocked with furniture and the other things necessary to make the homes fairly comparable to contemporary English homes. Even pottery found a welcome market in the islands. The Ironmongers, also, received impetus from this trade. A member of the Lords' Committee in 1787 commented that the trade was very "refreshing".[36] During the 1750's the manufacturers of checks, such as Thomas Touchet, were largely dependent on this branch of commerce. Between 1739 and 1759 most of the 70,000 pounds sterling worth of cotton piece goods sent to the British colonies went to the West Indies.[37] In 1774 one author declared that "Our manufactures are prodigiously increased, chiefly by the demand for them in our plantations, where they take off at least one half, and furnish us with many more valuable commodities for exportation... In short the advantages which redound to us from our American empire are not to be doubted"[38]

Among English families who acquired their fortunes through the West Indian Trade was that of W. E. Gladstone, the noted parliamentarian's father, one of the earliest to engage in the opening up of the trade to China, India and Russia, and it was the very first to send a vessel to Calcutta after the extension of the East Indian and China trades. The sugar and other produce that John Gladstone sold on the Liverpool market were grown on his own plantations and imported in his own ships.[39]

To determine the relative value of the colonial trade as compared with that "neglected" would involve sheer guessing. Adam Smith admitted that the new produce and the new capital maintained more productive labor.[40] But this was true, Smith maintained, not because of, but in spite of the monopoly created by the Navigation Acts.[41] Lord Sheffield felt that the plantation system had been abused.[42] Anderson thought that the traders "...had entirely frustrated, by the trade they carried on, the original intent of our planting those colonies, viz., to be a benefit to the mother country to which they owe their being and protection".[43] Concerning the general colonial set-up Adam Smith wrote:[44] "But in the system of laws which has been established for the management of our American and West Indian colonies, the interest of the home consumer has been sacrificed to that of the producer... A great empire has been established "for the sole purpose of raising up a nation of customers... For this purpose only, in the last two wars, more than a hundred and seventy millions in debt has been contracted... The interest of this debt alone is not only greater than the whole extraordinary profit which...was made by the monopoly of the colony trade, but than the whole value of that act (sic.) or than the whole value of the goods, which at an average have been annually exported to the colonies".[45] It is clear that Smith, a product of an entirely different age from that when mercantilist thinking held full sway, could not wholly appreciate the mercantilist point of view. When Smith wrote, capitalism was well on its way to maturity, and the institutions which had erected that system were becoming incompatible with its necessary concomitant, free trade.

At the basis of this trade on which capitalism was erected was Negro labor.[46] This labor supply, treated as so much capital,[47] was less costly than free labor;[48] and it was also the only labor suited for the purpose of exploiting the Islands, unless, indeed, it had been possible to persuade African natives to come to the plantations as free wage laborers. The slave system was clung to as long as economic circumstances permitted. Even Pitt who exercised his best oratory against slavery as Bissett put it:[49] "As a speculative philanthropist seeking emancipation, Mr. Pitt was one person; as the practical statesman, rejoicing that his country had acquired a new means of riches and power, in colonies, the cultivation of which would cause a much greater demand for negro slaves than before, Mr. Pitt was another person."[50] A Captain Denham testified to a committee of the House of Lords that "..... I think it is perfectly evident that it (the slave trade) must last to perpetuity.... and that its only limit would be the numbers Africa could supply." But institutions were changing, and the slave system was doomed to vanish with other mercantilist institutions.

CONCLUSION

The African trade was a very important factor in the growth of the capitalist economy in England. First, it furnished a considerable market for British manufactures, particularly textiles which exchanged for Africa's chief product, Negro slaves. We have noted, for example, the important role which Liverpool shipping played as a stimulus to Manchester manufacturing. Second, African gold was an important source of the medium of exchange which the rising capitalism of England demanded. Third, the great profits derived from the African trade, in spite of notorious losses, helped to build the large personal fortunes which eventually were turned from purely commercial to industrial employment. Finally, the African trade stimulated such industries as shipbuilding, and thus was an important factor in bringing about England's supremacy in the overseas trade.

The West Indian plantation economy, forming the final and most important apex of the triangle, was also important in the development of English capitalism. The West Indies furnished, to some extent at least, an outlet for British manufactures. But, more important than this, the plantations were an important source of raw materials. From the exploitation of slave labor in the West Indian economy, large fortunes arose. Some of this wealth was transferred to the mother country, and eventually invested in industrial enterprise.

For the development of the African trade and the West Indian plantations, the Negro slave was indispensable. Without slavery the African market could never have become the important outlet for British manufactures as it was in the eighteenth century. For it was with slaves primarily that Africa paid for European goods. In the West Indies, as we have seen, the labor supply brought from the west coast of Africa was the only type of manpower upon which the plantation system could thrive. For it was the only source of continuous, subsistence labor which the plantation demands in contradistinction to the intermittent supply required by industrial activity.

Without the Negro slave it is likely that neither the African trade nor the West Indian economy could have played an important part in the development of English capitalism; and hence it is unlikely that without the slave trade, English capitalism could have shown the phenomenal growth it did.

Footnotes

Chapter I

1. See Arthur L. Cross; "History of England and Greater Britain", New York, 1917, ch. 36, PP. 618-619.

2. "Plantation Work the Work of This Generation", London, 1682.

3. "Plaine Pathway to Plantations", London 1624.

4. Cf. "Purveyance in England Under Elizabeth", L. M. Spears, Journal of Political Economy." Vol. 24, pp. 755-774.

5. Cf. Postlethwayte, M. "The African Trade, Pillar and Support", London, 1745.

6. Such aid served more firmly to establish absolutism, but at the same time it created a strong bourgeoisie, the very force that was to overthrow monarchism.

7. See Richard Hakluyt, "Navigations, Voyages, Traffiques and Discoveries", Edinburgh edition of 1889, Vol. 11, p. 304. Also Vol. 5, pp. 200-321.

8. This philosophy is epitomized in Jacques Savary's "Le Parfait Negociant", Paris, 1675. Cobert is said to have collaborated in this work.

9. "Das Merkantilsystem in Seiner Historischen Bedeutung", Leipzig, 1880.

10. "Encyclopedia of the Social Sciences", 1933 edition, p. 338. Vol. X.

11. Cf. Professor Abram L. Harris, "The Negro as Capitalist", p. 3.

Chapter II

1. "History of the British West Indies", (5 vols) London, 1819. Vol. 2 p.43.

2. Ibid., vol. 2. p. 44.

3. Robert Bisset, "History of the Slave Trade" (2 vols) London, 1805. I, 27.

4. Op. cit., vol. 11, p. 69.

5. Edwards, op. cit. vol. 2 p. 47.

6. A. G. Smith, "William Cecil", London, 1934. pp. 130-131.

7. Edwards, op. cit., vol. 2, p. 51.

8. Hakluyt, op. cit., vol. 11, p. 304.

9. Cross, op. cit., p. 296.

10. Bisset, op. cit., vol. 1., p. 30.

11. Roger Coke, "A Discourse on Trade", London 1670, preface.

12. "Trade Revived", Anon. London, 1659.

13. H. Meredith, "The Raoyal African Company", London, 1812, p. 246.

14. See Painter, Gorges, et al, "Answer of the Company of Royal Adventurers",
    London, 1667, who maintained that the profits from the trade were
    not the main reason for purchasing the almost worthless stock, but
    that it was the 'indirect' advantages.

15. Malachy Postlethwayte, "Universal Dictionary of Trade and Commerce",
    3d edition, London, 1766, vol. 2. p. 10.

16. "Constitution and Management of the Trade to Africa", London, 1709.

17. Postlethwayte, op. cit. vol. 1, p. 11.

18. Ibid., vol. 2. p. 10.

19. Anon. "Detection of Proceedings and Practices of the Directors of the
    Royal Africa Company". London, 1749, p. 8.

20. Op. cit. vol. 1. pp. 7 - 15.

21. Much of this was Franch brandy re-exported. See Capt. William Snelgrave,
    "An Account of Guinea", London, 1754.

22. Op. cit. vol. 2. p. 16.

23. Ibid. vol. 2. p. 41.

24. Ibid. vol. 2. p. 42.

25. "Detection of Proceedings, etc", p. 9.

26. "The African Trade, Pillar and Support", p. 36.

27. John Hippisley, "Essays on Africa", London, 1764. p. 41.

28. Ibid., p. 26.

29. "Dictionary", vol. 2. p. 23.

30. L.C.A. Knowles, "The Industrial and Commercial Revolutions in Great
    Britain", London, 1926, p. 343.

31. This trade started from England, moved to Africa, thence to the West
    Indies returning to England. It involved articles of British manufacture,
    East India goods, slaves, ivory, gold, sugar, rum, rice, tobacco, and
    other West Indian products as the chief commodities.

32. I.e., old gold.

33. A. P. Wadsworth and Julia L. Mann, "The Cotton Trade and Industrial
    Lancashire", London, 1931. p. 230.

34. Hays, (?)   "The Importance of Supporting the Royal African Company",
    London, 1745.

35. "Detection of Proceedings, etc." p. 3.

36. Hays, Op. cit. p. 19.

37. "The Cotton Trade, etc." p. 3.

38. Snelgrave, op. cit. p. 2.

39. Ibid. p. 193.

40. Gomer Williams, "History of the Liverpool Privateers", Liverpool, 1897,
    p. 467.

41. Edwards, op. cit. vol. 2, Appendix 2, p. 226.

42. John Lattimer, "Annals of Bristol in the 17th Century", Bristol, 1900.
    p. 474

43. Ibid. p. 485.

44. For accounts of Bristol ships built especially for this trade see (1)
    William Barrett, "History of Bristol", Bristol, 1789, and (2) Damer
    Powell, "Bristol Privateers and Ships of War", Bristol, 1930.

45. John Lattimer, "Annals of Bristol in the 18th Century", Bristol, 1893,
    p. 472.

46. Ibid. p. 462.

47. "Annals of Bristol in the 17th Century", p. 350.

48. Williams, op. cit., pp. 467. ff.

49. "The Cotton Trade, etc", p. 179.

50. Ibid., p. 224.

51. Ibid., p. 224.

52. Williams, op. cit., p. 473.

53. Edwards, op. cit., vol. 2, p. 226.

54. "The Cotton Trade, etc.", p. 228.

55. Ibid. p. 146. The figures are: Africa, 39, 129 to 98,696; West Indies, 57, 134 to 66,713.

56. Ibid., p. 225.

57. He might, however, buy some on his own. The shipmasters frequently did so.

58. "The Cotton Trade, etc.," p. 230.

59. Ibid. p. 230.

60. Williams, op. cit., p. 598.

61. Ibid., p. 617.

62. "The Cotton Trade, etc.", p. 228.

63. Compiled from Williams, Edwards, Bisset's and Postlethwayte's examples.

64. Cunliffe was a leading merchant, owning property in the West Indies, and a partner in a Manchester handloom concern, while his brother Walter was a director of the Bank of England. See Leo. H. Grindon, "Manchester Banks and Bankers", Manchester, 1878; H. H. Bassett, "Men of Note..", London, 1900; and H. R. Fox Browne, "English Merchants", London, 1866, vol. 2 p. 120.

64. Williams. op. cit., p. 679

65. D. Defoe, "A Tour Through the Whole Island of Great Britain" (4 vols) London, 1753, 5th ed., vol. 3, pp. 202-3.

66. W. Enfield, "An Essay towards the History of Liverpool", Warrington, 1773 p. 25, et al.

67. J. Aiken, "A Description of the Country around Manchester", London, 1795, p. 335.

68. "The Cotton Trade, etc." p. 231.

69. Ibid. p. 243.

70. Ibid. p. 151.

71. A. Ure, "The Cotton Manufacture of Great Britain", London, 1836. Vol. 1, p. 209-11.

72. Aiken, op. cit. p. 521.

73. Ibid, pp. 158-161.

74. "The Cotton Trade, etc.", p. 288.

75. Ibid., pp. 151-154.

76. See T. Baines and W. Fairbairn, "Lancashire and Cheshire..." (2 vols), London, 1869.

77. Williams, op. cit., p. 598.

78. Ibid., p. 599.

79. Ibid., pp. 599-600.

80. Postlethwayte, "Dictionary", Vol. 2. p. 16 for 1680-1688; Edwards. op. cit. Vol. 2. p. 226, for 1701-1780. Wadsworth and Mann, op. cit. are in virtual agreement.

81. "Economic Writings of Sir William Petty", Hull ed., Cambridge, 1899. p. 296.

82. Postlethwayte, op. cit., vol. 2. p. 42.

83. "The Cotton Trade, etc"., p. 231.

84. Hakluyt, op. cit. vol. 11, pp. 100-101.

85. Ibid., p. 102.

86. Ibid., p. 102.

87. Ibid., p. 103.

88. Ibid., pp. 152-195.

89. Ibid. p. 195.

90. Ibid. p. 127.

91. Ibid. p. 69

92. Ibid. p. 73.

93. Ibid. pp. 84-90

94. Ibid. p. 312.

95. Ibid. p. 321.

96. Ibid. p. 331.

97. Calendar of State Papers, Colonial Series, London, 1880, vol. 5, (Preface) p. 28.

Chapter III

1. "Wealth of nations", Cannon edition, New York edition, 1937, book 4. p. 525.

2. Smith's doubt was due to his fight against monopoly (Ibid. p. 564), as against his certainty of the Utility of the trade itself. See pp. 573-75, 576-78, Ibid.

3. "Misere de la Philosophie", in "Gesamtausgabe", Band six, p. 181. (Berlin, 1932).

4. Robert Bissett, op. cit., vol. 2, p. 313.

5. See Frank W. Pittman, "Slavery on the British West India Plantation". Journal of Negro History, October, 1926. pp. 584-668.

6. "Account of the Island of Jamaica" (2 vols), London, 1790, vol. II. p. 310.

7. "The African Trade, etc.", pp. 13, 14.

8. Edwards, op. cit., vol. II, p. 150.

9. Ibid., vol. II, p. 157.

10. Cal. State Papers, vol. 5, Pref. p. 85.

11. Ibid. vol. 5, paragraph 618.

12. Cal. State Papers, vol. 7. Par. 144.

13. Ibid. vol. 7, Pref. p. 22.

14. F. Cundall, "Governors of Jamaica in the Seventeenth Century". London, 1936. p. 21.

15. Cal. State Papers. vol. 7, p. 99.

16. Lowell J. Ragatz, "The Fall of the Planter Class in the British Caribbean, 1763-1833", New York, 1928 esp. p. 44.

17. Cal. State Papers, vol. 7., para. 126.

18. R. C. Dallas, "History of the Maroons", (2 vols), London, 1803. Vol 1. p. 64.

19. Ibid. vol. 2. p. 373.

20. Ibid. vol. 1, p. 65.

21. See Ragatz, op. cit. pp. 42, ff.

22. "Twelve Letters on Hindrances to Trade", Bristol, 1820.

23. Alexander MacDonnell, "Colonial Commerce", London, 1828, pp. 14, ff.

24. The Vicissitudes of the trade are vividly described in William Stouts' "Autobiography of William Stout", Harland Edition, Lancashire, 1851.

25. Op. cit., vol. 2, pp. 275, ff.

26. Op. cit., vol. 2, p. 299.

27. Op. cit., vol. 2, pp. 156, ff.

28. Edwards, op. cit., vol. 2, p. 291.

29. "Dictionary of Commerce and Trade", vol. 1. p. 2.

30. "On the Assiento Trade", London, 1728. p. 30.

31. "Memoirs and Considerations...", (2 vols) London, 1740. Vol. 1. p. 18.

32. John Entick, "Present State of the British Empire. (5 vols) London, 1774. Vol. 4. p. 479.

33. Edwards, op. cit., vol. 2. p. 2.

34. My computation, a minimum composite of the figures from Edwards, Bissett and Postlethwayte.

35. T. Massie, "State of the British Sugar-Colony Trade", London, 1759, pp. 1-9.

36. "Report of...Lords of...Council on the Slave Trade", London, 1789. p.461.

37. "The Cotton Trade, etc.", p. 146.

38. Entick, op. cit. vol. 1. p. 110.

39. "Fortunes Made in Business", Various writers. (2 vols) London, 1884. Vol. 2. pp. 118, 123, 177.

40. Op. cit. pp. 431, ff.

41. See John Adolphus, "Political State of the British Empire. (3 vols) London 1818, vol. 3, pp. 166-170.

42. Strictures on the Necessity of...maintaining...the colonial System of Great Britain", London, 1806. p. 6.

43. "History of Commerce". (2 vols) London, 1819. vol. 2. p. 455.

44. Op. cit. p. 626, also, p. 550.

45. Op. cit. pp. 402. Cf. "Emancipation on Disguise", London, 1814, esp. p. 14.

46. Karl Marx commented: "In fact the veiled slavery of the wage-earners in Europe needed, for its pedestal, slavery pure and simple". "Capital" Kerr edition, Chicago, 1926. vol. 1. p. 833.

47. See James Stephens, "The Crisis of the Sugar Colonies", London, 1802 p. 33.

48. See M. Cary, "Slave Labor Employed in Manufactures", Phila. 1827 But compare: Sir Josiah Conder, "Wages or the Whip", London, 1833, pp. 2, 106.

49. Op. cit., Vol. 2, p. 223.

50. Pitt was a close friend of William Beckford, Jamaica planter. See Basil Williams, "Life of William Pitt", (2 vols) Esp. vol. 1. p. 158, London, 1913.

NEGRO DISFRANCHISEMENT IN VIRGINIA

By Robert E. Martin

* * * * ──────────────────────────────────── * * * *

CHAPTER I

Introduction

This essay was originally designed to embrace a study of the movement to disfranchise the Negro in Virginia and South Carolina during the
period 1867-1937. The author had accordingly planned to trace the general
course of this movement which involved the early phases of coercion and
intimidation; the transition period between Reconstruction and disfranchisement by legislative and constitutional provision; and, finally, the
period in which "white supremacy" triumphed by way of the "white primary."
However, in the course of the study it was discovered that the materials were
too voluminous for a single essay and that the two states presented such
different situations that it was thought best to confine the work primarily
to Virginia. A brief comparison of the two states will show the wisdom of
this plan and, at the same time, furnish a background for a more detailed
examination of Virginia politics from 1867-1937.

In the first place, the population of Virginia consisted of many
more whites than Negroes. The Census of 1870 reported that of the 1,225,163
total inhabitants in the State, 712,089 were white and 512,841 colored. On
the other hand, the majority of the people of South Carolina was colored.[1]
According to the Census of 1870 there were 415,814 Negroes in that State as
compared with 289,667 whites.[2] As already noted conditions in the two States
during the period of Congressional Reconstruction were entirely dissimilar.

Between 1867-76, South Carolina was under a revolutionary "dictatorship" composed of black and white democratic elements. But Virginia never had a so-called "Negro-scallywag-carpetbagger" government. Nor was Virginia ever faced with a threat of "black domination," although on several occasions this was alleged to be the case and the allegation was used with telling political effect.

The return to power of the old regimes in South Carolina and Virginia was vastly different. In South Carolina the first phase of Reconstruction was characterized by the complete control of black and white Republicans. This was followed by the split in Republican ranks, after which came the reign of terror instituted by the reactionary white element which resulted in a counter-revolutionary coup d'etat and the establishment of a dual government for the State. Finally the old powers triumphed and Wade Hampton, aided by the recall of the northern army, was put back at the head of the State. All this, plus the bloody battles, the Negro militias, the Ku Klux Klan terrorism, etc., was vastly different from the return to power of the old regime in Virginia. It is true that the Old Dominion witnessed intimidation and corruption but it never paralleled that of South Carolina and the other States in the lower South. In Virginia after two years of extremely mild military occupation, the old leaders returned to power in the first election. And thus as early as 1869 the traditional leadership of the Old Dominion could celebrate the "restoration" of the State, whereas a similar victory was not achieved in South Carolina until 1876.

In pursuing this study, the author has become convinced that the political events in Virginia can best be understood when viewed in the perspective of the class composition of the State. It is true that racial factors frequently beclouded essentially class issues, thereby preventing rational class alignments. But this constant intrusion of the racial factor is explicable from the standpoint of class antagonisms. Thus the vital phases of the movement described in this paper are directly traceable to the conflicting interests in stratified southern society before the Civil War and its confused but revolutionary aftermath.

In establishing its hegemony over the national economy, the North found it necessary to make the Negro its political ally. By virtue of his alliance with the middle class North, the Negro helped to consumate the bourgeois-democratic revolution of 1860-1877. In this transformation the Negro was made a citizen and accorded the democratic rights of man. Yet, as important as these gains were, they were never realized for the whole of the Negro race, mainly because the old plantation system was never completely uprooted.[3] Thus without property the Negro's legal and political rights were rendered fictitious. And in time even his theoretical citizenship was taken away from him by disfranchisement and intimidation. Virginia is to be viewed, therefore, in the light of the forces which have prevented the carrying through of the democratic innovations which came with the triumph of industrialism over the slave regime.

It will not be necessary to enter into a discussion of the rightness or wrongness of the so-called "Negro-scallywag-carpetbagger" governments which were set up during the period of Radical Reconstruction, as Virginia never was ruled by such at any time. In the brief interim between the institution of Congressional Reconstruction and the restoration of the state to the old leadership, Virginia was under a mild military rule.[4] However, it must be said that the writer is not in agreement with those who brand the black and white Reconstruction governments as being the awful rule of "densely ignorant blacks and completely unscrupulous whites." The constitutions and laws framed by these bodies disprove such allegations. Dr. DuBois, however, has stated the case for these governments in a most effective manner. His book, "<u>Black Reconstruction</u>, refutes the accounts of such books as Claude Bowers' <u>Tragic Era</u>, J. W. Burgess' <u>Reconstruction</u> <u>and</u> <u>the</u> <u>Constitution</u>, and J. F. Rhodes' <u>History</u> <u>of</u> <u>the</u> <u>United</u> <u>States</u>.

Under a system of industrial democracy based on popular suffrage, free access to the ballot is absolutely necessary to the protection of any group in the enjoyment of its rights. Today, especially in view of Fascism's threat to engulf the world, political power and the full participation in democratic processes of government are absolutely essential to economic security. Thus this paper is devoted to a study of suffrage in a local situation, from two aspects: first, in relation to the matter of group rights under a theoretical democracy; and second, in relation to the relief it can offer to the needs and aspirations of an essentially working class group. The author believes, in the words of Montesquieu, that

> It is plain... that if the government, whether state or federal, controls or disposes of suffrage, or allows it to be disposed of, without warrant in the constitution, it strikes at the very vitals of the republic from which it derives its entire existence and power.

CHAPTER II

POLITICAL BACKGROUND, 1861 - 1867

As in the other thirteen original States, sectionalism has played a
vital role in Virginia politics since the beginning of its history. The
struggle between the Tidewater region and the mountainous sections of the West
began in the first Constitutional Convention of 1776 and continued unabated
until the Civil War.[1] While the eastern section of Virginia was synonymous
with prestige and power as in the other thirteen States, its wealth and
political influence was not derived from banking, commerce and speculation as
was the case above the Mason and Dixon line. The power of eastern or Tidewater
Virginia rested upon the slave economy which was made possible by the rich
lands of this section. This section augmented its political power by counting
the slaves in the apportionment of representatives and, thus, on the basis of
the white population, had a disproportionate share of the representation. This
practice was always opposed by the non-slaveholding whites of the western part
of the State. The height of the conflict between East and West, between the
"highlands" and "lowlands" in Virginia, was reached in 1861 when the West
declined to follow the eastern aristocrats in the rebellion against the national
government.

At the convention called to decide the question of secession, the
delegates from the Northwest section opposed withdrawal from the Union.[2] The
westerners took separate action and began a movement to set up a new government in Virginia. Subsequently, June 11, 1861, a new state administration was
established at Wheeling. After declaring vacant all State offices held by the
secessionists, loyal officials were elected, with Travis H. Pierpont as
governor. Pierpont's government remained in Wheeling until the movement for

the establishment of a new State, separate from Virginia, resulted in the creation of West Virginia. The "restored government of Virginia" was then removed to Alexandria.[3]

This "shadowy" organization, recognized by Lincoln as the government of all Virginia, continued at Alexandria from 1863 until 1865, when it was transferred, in May, to Richmond, thus supplanting the Confederate administration which had operated up to Lee's surrender.[4] On the 9th of May, President Johnson, Mr. Lincoln's successor, proclaimed the Pierpont administration to be the legal government of Virginia.

The Governor at once called a meeting of the legislature and began plans for the rehabilitation of the State. In response to his appeal, the legislature passed an enabling act designed to repeal the clauses of the 1864 Constitution which disfranchised many of those who had aided the rebellion.[5] At the conclusion of its sessions, the Speaker congratulated the members of the Assembly for their timely action which had kept the State government out of the control of the "Abolitionists." Continuing, he declared; "Virginia is now safe. Whatever they may do to other states, they cannot force a provisional government upon her. Whatever they may do to other states, thank God, they cannot now saddle negro suffrage upon us."[6]

In pursuing his policy of reorganizing local government in the State, Governor Pierpont became very lenient and conciliatory in his attitude toward those who had been active in Confederate ranks. In the election at Richmond in July 1865, ex-Confederate officers were elected to the positions of mayor, commonwealth's attorney and superintendent of the almshouse.[7] This action caused considerable resentment among Union sympathizers and their protest led to the nullification of the election. Pierpont's policy of conciliation toward the Confederates soon drew the bitter condemnation of the local Radicals. It was charged before the Congressional Committee that was investigating conditions in the South that "the loyal men of the State are being totally sacrificed and turned over to the power of the secessionists."[8]

Fearing the return of the rebels to power, the Radicals met at Alexandria in June 1865, and organized a "political association." At this Convention the following resolutions were adopted:

(1) That it was essential to prevent Virginia from coming into the control of the secessionists; (2) that it seemed as if this control might be gained; (3) that the Constitution of Virginia should be amended so as to confer the right of suffrage upon, and restrict it to, loyal male citizens without regard to color.[9]

As Eckenrode points out, "This was the first announcement of the advocacy of negro suffrage by the Republican party in Virginia."[10]

The fall elections of 1865 confirmed Republican apprehension that the state was rapidly passing out of their control. The constitution of 1864 was amended to give the legislature power to return the franchise "to rebels and their aiders and abettors." And the state legislature was filled with men who were able to take the test oath. No Republican was elected to Congress.

In the meantime, opposition to President Johnson's "mild" reconstruction policy was developing in the United States Congress.[11] We can dismiss as ungermane to our study any discussion of the conflict between Johnson and the Radical Republicans in Congress in their plans for reconstructing the South. As interesting as the story is, it has been described by many authors.[12] It is sufficient for our purposes that the rebellious states, during this period of local autonomy, 1865 - 1867, were rapidly reestablishing conditions which were remarkably similar to those that existed under the slave regime. Men only recently in arms against the authority of the United States government were in numerous instances placed in control of

local government and were seeking their former seats in Congress. All the
while the Negro was being rapidly reduced to a political and economic condition that differed but little from slavery.

"Black Codes," requiring every Negro to be in the service of some
white person, were being written into law by most of the secession states.
Vagrancy laws were enacted, exacting severe penalties from all Negroes who
were found "unlawfully assembling" and/or who refused to work for "usual and
common" wages.[13] The non-payment of poll taxes levied on all ablebodied
Negroes constituted prima facie evidence of vagrancy.[14] It was even proposed
in a party convention in South Carolina, that the legislature exercise the
powers to

> restrain negroes and persons of color... from engaging in any
> species of traffic, in any other department of labor than menial
> service, agriculture, mining, roadmaking, and the production of
> naval stores and employments incidental to these...."[15]

It is evident that "The South's plans for transition legislation looked rather
towards continued subordination of the Negro, "freedman' though he might
technically be."[16]

President Johnson's seven months supremacy was brought to an abrupt
end as Congress, on December 4, 1865, refused to seat the southern representatives. Irrespective of this rebuff, Virginia failed to attempt to con-
ciliate the rapidly developing Radical sentiment in Congress. It proceeded
with a program which was quite similar to that of other secessionist states.
The Assembly, on December 8, removed the suffrage restrictions imposed on
ex-Confederates. Then the legislature pushed through the vagrancy bill.[17]
This statute provided that vagrants were to be hired out for terms not
exceeding three months and gave the employers the power to deduct the cost
of up-keep from their wages. If a vagrant ran away, his employer was

entitled to a month's free service in addition to the specified time. He
could be worked with ball and chain after such an attempt.[18] In the event
his employer refused to reemploy him, the vagrant was to be put into public
service, or he might be confined in jail on bread and water.

Such a measure naturally resulted in a form of peonage.[19] On January
24, 1866, General Terry, the military commander, knowing that the landholders
in many sections had combined to keep wages down, issued orders that the act
was not to be enforced against "any colored person in this department."[20]
General Terry's reasons for voiding the Bill were expressed as follows:

> In many counties of this State, meetings of employers have been
> entered into for the purpose of depressing the wages of the
> freedmen below the real value of their labor, far below the
> prices formerly paid to masters for labor performed by their
> slaves.... It places the freedmen wholly in the power of their
> employers....
>
> The ultimate effect of the statute will be to reduce the freed-
> men to a condition of servitude worse than that from which they
> have been emancipated-- a condition which will be slavery in all
> but its name.[21]

Alarmed by the determination of the rebel states to nullify the emancipation
and to return the aristocratic leadership again to power, Congress initiated
an investigation of these States. Many northern people felt that since the
southern governments had rejected the opportunity to show good faith sterner
measures should be taken against them.

In a meeting at Alexandria in February, 1866, the Republicans asked
Congress to declare the existing government of Virginia to be provisional and
to establish a territorial administration for the protection of those loyal
to the Union. Five months later a convention was held and the Republican
party of Virginia was formally organized.[22] The convention advocated the
disfranchisement of ex-Confederates and a restricted Negro suffrage limited
by law.[23]

Several events transpired to further increase sentiment for radical reconstruction of Virginia. Congress, in defiance of Johnson, passed the Freedmen's Bureau and the Civil Rights Bills in 1866. On April 16 of that year, a white mob attempted to break up a parade of Negroes at Norfolk, in celebration of the passage of the Civil Rights Bill. In the riot that resulted, two whites and two Negroes were killed. In consequence martial law was declared.[24] Shortly afterwards, a Judge at Alexandria rendered a decision contrary to the Civil Rights Bill. A colored witness was brought forth to testify in a suit, but the Judge decided that the "laws of Virginia forbade negro testimony in cases where only white men were parties, and that Congressional law cannot impair the rights of the state to decide the competency of witnesses."[25] Another incident which further aroused feeling against the administration in Virginia occurred in November 1866, when a white man, Doctor J. L. Watson, killed a Negro in Rockbridge County. Although circumstances indicated that the act was without justification, the state court acquitted Watson. He was rearrested on order of General Schofield, acting under authority of the act of Congress of July 16, 1866, and held for military trial. General Schofield subsequently refused to acknowledge a writ of habeas corpus which had been issued by the Circuit Court of Richmond. Nevertheless, President Johnson released Watson, for which he was roundly criticized.[26]

The Virginia Assembly convened in its second session on December 2, 1866. The Governor, apprehensive of the ominous clouds forming over Washington, strongly urged that a policy of conciliation be adopted, the harsh laws aimed at the Negro be modified, and that the 14th Amendment be ratified.[27] The legislature, however, supported by a bitterly outspoken press, refused to accept the Fourteenth Amendment.[28] The vote of rejection was 27 to 0 in

the senate and 74 to 1 in the lower chamber.[29]   Later the legislature was
more disposed to ratify the Amendment and probably would have done so; but
it was too late, as Congress, on March 2, 1867, passed the first of the
Reconstruction Acts.[30]   Virginia became Military District Number One.[31]
But General John M. Schofield, who was placed in command of the District,
promised that he would "supercede the civil authorities only in so far as
it was necessary to discharge his duties."[32]   This promise did not forbode
good for the Negro in the politics of the State.

CHAPTER III

THE NEGRO ENTERS POLITICS

Congress, by the Acts of March 2 and March 27, 1867, had provided for the reorganization of the governments of the seceded states. The officers in charge of each military district were instructed to take before the first of the following September, a registration of all persons entitled to vote. Following this an election was to be held to provide for the calling of a constitutional convention and to elect delegates to the same.[1]

General Schofield, Commander of the Virginia area, carried out Congressional instructions and called for registration of all male citizens except such ex-Confederates as were disqualified by the Fourteenth Amendment and the Virginia Constitution of 1864.[2] At the end of the registration period there were 225,933 names on the books. Of these 120,101 were white and 105,832 were Negro registrants.[3] The Republicans had planned to set up the new state governments on a basis of universal Negro suffrage and the size of the black registration in Virginia reflected a warm approval of this action by the newly freed Negroes.

Although the whites had a numerical majority of 14,269, the Negro vote was more strategic. The whites were in a majority in 52 counties.[4] The fifty counties having more blacks than whites were in the more populous southern and eastern sections. In the latter counties there were 125,895 registrants, whereas the counties having white majorities contained only 90,555. And therefore, on the basis of the apportionment, one delegate to 2,061 constituents,[5] the Negroes had the advantage.

The election to decide the convention issue was set for October 18, 19 and 20, 1867[6], but before describing this great event in the history of

Virginia, it is necessary briefly to examine the frame of mind and the
attitudes of the white people of the Old Dominion in regard to the Negro
and his newly acquired position as a voter. And in so doing one can better
understand the attitudes toward calling a convention, the organic law which
it was to promulgate and the events subsequent to it.

As soon as it became evident that Congress was not going to tolerate
an immediate return to power of the old leadership, there was bitter
reaction in the aristocratic circles of Virginia, as well as in the other
secessionist states.[7] And when Negro suffrage loomed up as inevitable,
this cry became intensified. However, opposition to admitting the Negro to
suffrage did not prevail among all of the whites of Virginia. There was a
considerable number who were willing to accept Negro suffrage as a fact and
to join with the freedmen in working for the rehabilitation of the state.
Those thus tolerantly, if not favorably, disposed consisted of two groups.
There were, on the one hand, a large number of small farmers and middle-
class Virginians who had long been struggling against planter domination and
who were not adverse to combining with the Negro to prevent the reestablishment of aristocratic hegemony. It is true that some of the people of this
category feared that the Negroes would vote with their former masters,[8] but
the heavy Negro vote for the convention and subsequent events did much to
remove the fear on this score. The other group which did not oppose Negro
suffrage at first was made up of a large section of the old leaders and
aristocrats. They felt that their former slaves, ignorant and in need of
protection, could easily be secured to support their cause and follow their
leadership.[9]

Since so many whites were disposed to accept the new dispensation,
there sprang up a strong indigenous movement for racial cooperation. For

a while it seemed that there was some chance of racial ranks being closed and mutual effort being made to rebuild the economy of the State. During the middle of April, 1867, a large mass meeting was held at the Court House Square in Petersburg at which a desire to work in this direction was expressed. At the meeting, of which the Richmond Dispatch wrote: "The crowd was immense, and the whites and blacks mixed up indiscriminately, and the best disposition was manifested by all present,"[10] it was decided that equal legal and political rights should obtain for both races. Resolutions advocating political equality and the equitable provision of educational opportunities for white and colored were also adopted. Several inter-racial conventions adopted these resolutions as the movement for racial cooperation spread throughout the State.[11]

An indication that the Negroes were not adverse to joining in the movement for mutual effort is shown in the action of groups of them at Richmond inviting several prominent white men of that city to give them their political views. Three of those invited promptly responded and spoke at a meeting held in the local theatre.[12] Indicative of the spirit of solidarity which was trying to manifest itself was the following incident. At a convention held in the African Church in Richmond, April 17, 1867, two hundred and ten delegates, fifty of whom were white, adopted the following resolution:

> That we recognize the great fact that the interests of the laboring classes of the State are identical, and that without regard to color, we desire to elevate them to their true position.[13]

The above and similar events probably cannot be used to show any overwhelming desire on the part of the whites to accord the Negro complete equality and accept him as a recently found brother, nor that the Negro expected or sought such. An even slight acquaintance with conditions obtaining in Virginia prior to 1860 in which the Negro had faced the necessity of accepting the status of a subordinate--an inferior [14]-- would prevent one from taking this view. However, this movement did represent, it would seem, a growing sense of tolerance between the races, an attitude of mutual dependency, a feeling that progress for each was dependent upon mutual effort.

This movement for racial collaboration, however, was not to progress undisturbed. It was destined to be aborted by the circumstances growing out of the conflicting nature of southern society. Its development was arrested by a reactionary program, begun by the former aristocratic leaders and politicians and carried through by classes in the lower social strata. These "Bourbon" forces had in great part been disfranchised and thus put at a tremendous disadvantage in the new order. And it was necessary, if they were to survive, to regain their old position and status. In the old order, the aristocrats had been able to maintain their domination by means of a highly qualified suffrage, limited by stiff property qualifications. But now that bourgeois forces had revolutionized things and forced an extension of democracy downwards, it was necessary to control a larger voting power. Therefore, cognizant of the historical antipathy between their class and the small farmers, the growing middle class and the masses of poor whites, they sought to secure the support of the Negroes.

With magnanimous flair they proffered their leadership to the thousands of newly enfranchised freedmen.[15] Conservative ranks were thrown open and the Negro welcomed by those who had always been his "friends."[16] The old leadership saw the influx of black and white Republicans from the North and were trying hard to counteract any radical propaganda they might bring.

Some of the upper class leaders even went so far as to seek admission into Republican ranks. They felt, of course, that once on the inside, they would neutralize the "invidious" effect of the "scalywags" and "carpet-baggers" and thereby gain control of the party. Accordingly, a convention of white Conservatives[17] of Albemarle County, through resolutions, expressed the desire to "cooperate with the party that will give us protection of life and property, and believing that the Republican party of the United States alone has the power to give us protection, we desire to cooperate with them."[18]

The newspaper, the Richmond Whig, led the movement to accept the situation, subscribe to the Congressional Reconstruction policy and restore the state to the Union through the agency of the Republican party.[19]

The Radical Republican leaders, however, hotly opposed admitting the reactionaries into their ranks. They knew that should these forces get in they would begin at once to try to gain control of the Party and attempt to tone the movement down. This, they realized, would spell the end for the militant leaders. And men like James W. Hunnicutt, the most outspoken native white Virginia Republican, counseled the Negroes to be wary of the men who had become so quickly "converted" to Republican principles.

As the election approached almost every means was used to cower the Negroes into repudiating the convention. The press daily carried warnings that the Negro had better not pursue the "suicidal" course of voting for the convention and supporting radical candidates. The Enquirer and Examiner declared that

> If the negroes are such fools as to vote for "Hunnicut and his set" against the respectable, talented and well-known gentlemen who have been nominated in this city, their present employers should forthwith set them adrift ....
> They are not fit to be employed in the houses and factories of respectable gentlemen.

The following editorial is typical of the unrestrained temper of the
Virginia newspapers:

> The white men of this State...will resist to the death the dom-
> ination of the negro, and will defy and trample upon any organic
> law or statute which essays to make the white man the inferior
> of the black. There is no power which can force a white majority
> to endure the Africanization of their State, when they have the
> physical power to prevent it. The horrors, therefore, of resist-
> ance to negro rule can only be secured by voting the Conservative
> ticket.[21]

The reactionaries thus alternated between threatening the Negro, on
the one hand, and posing as his friend on the other. Just before election
day the Whig carried more than a dozen of the following quotations inter-
spersed through its editorial page:

> COLORED MEN: Remember that those who own all the property
> can get along without your assistance, but that you cannot
> get along without theirs.
> ....
> COLORED MEN: Don't give your employers reason to believe
> that you are hostile to them and that they can get along
> better without you than with you.
> ....
> COLORED MEN: Winter is at hand. How many of you have
> houses of your own, and fuel and meat and meal laid up?
> To whom do you look for the means of providing these?[22]

Every possible argument was given to show that the only logical thing
the Negro could do was to support Conservatism. The Negro, however, was not
over enthusiastic about following the leadership of his former oppressors.
They were dubious about placing their faith, their confidence, and, in the
last analysis, their future, into the hands of those who had owned and treated
them as chattels. They had not forgotten that only a year or two before the
old leaders had attempted to restore a system of peonage which, but for the
intervention of the military, acting on Republican orders, would have been
successful. And so the Negroes, ignoring for the most part, the counsel of
the "rebel aristocracy," went into the elections of 1867--their first political

campaign--as a unit. Casting the threats of the whites aside, the Negroes
gave wholehearted sanction to the convention. Disappointed at the action of
the freedmen, the Enquirer and Examiner triumphantly noted that

> those negroes who voted that ticket /Radical/ yesterday, and
> last night were promptly informed that their services were
> not wanted any longer. This is perfectly proper, and if it
> had been universally done from the beginning of the negro
> political troubles, this city would not have been disgraced
> by the mobs of howling negroes who have made the nights
> hideous.[23]

The Negroes, however, were not deterred. They believed that a convention should be held and voted for men whom they thought would do a good
job of liberalizing the organic law of the Old Dominion.

As to calling a constitutional convention, 107,342 votes were cast
in favor of and 61,887 in opposition to such action.[24] Only 14,835 whites
voted for the convention, whereas, only 638 Negroes voted against it.[25]
These figures illustrate the racial nature of the vote for the convention.
The Negroes, realizing that the calling of a convention would result in an
extension of rights to the freedmen, were for it almost solidly. The whites,
many (39,073) of whom failed to vote on the issue, hoped to show disapproval
of the pending action.[26] There was, however, considerable white sentiment
in favor of the convention.[27] The Republicans, or "Radicals" as they were
called, after the militant Congressional group, elected 70 members, 25 of whom
were Negroes, to the proposed convention; the Conservatives, 35.[28]

Reaction to this victory by the Republicans was instantaneous. The
"rebel aristocracy" had been defeated, and liberals, black and white, were
going to play the decisive role in giving Virginia a new organic law. The
Negro, in spite of the determined bid made for his vote, had refused to
enroll under the banners of the old leadership. At once the cry of "negro
domination" went up. Although only 25 out of 105 delegates were Negroes,

the reactionaries played up the eminent "threat" of the "Africanization"[29] of Virginia. To upset the present, and prevent any future movement toward solidarity between small white farmers, middle class elements and the Negroes, the reactionaries began a serious campaign to alienate the races. They saw this incipient movement as a real threat to their dominance. And they were not slow in realizing that this tendency, if allowed to continue, would mean the inevitable development of a spirit of class consciousness and realization of class interest which would probably lead directly to class action. So the recalcitrants, unsuccessful in gaining the control of the black masses, and seeing large numbers of white voters deserting to Republican ranks, embarked on a campaign of "divide and rule."

They went forth into the land with the plea, and challenge, that "white supremacy" must be maintained, and that white civilization must be saved from "the barbarians."[30] This was, indeed, a potent weapon, which appealed to the ignorant whites. Too, the situation at that time was decidedly favorable to the creation and nourishment of racial animosities. The people, just out of the throes of a long, devastating war, were easy prey to the harangues of demagogues. The emotions of both races had been able to drop but little from the fever pitch of the bloody days of 1862-1865. And so the white man was told that the only possible way for Virginia to regain her spot in the sun was by "keeping the nigger in his place." The practical expression of this movement to keep the Negro "in his place" was the institution of methods and techniques designed to effect and maintain the social inferiority, the economic subordination, and the political impotence of the Negro people. And every means, from outright, overt intimidation and terrorism to so-called "legal" disfranchisement, was used to wrench the ballot from the black electorate.

It is quite likely that if the Negro had blindly followed the Conservative leadership, given them his vote, and never waivered in his loyalty to and support of his former rulers--which would have been the same as not having the franchise--this group would not have begun the agitation for black disfranchisement. As long as the Negroes should contribute and make possible aristocratic hegemony, there naturally would be no occasion for keeping him from the polls. An indication of what the blacks would have received in return for such support is found in the following quotation. Speaking of the offer of Conservative leadership and its refusal by the freedmen, a southern apologist states that, of course,

> The Negroes were not offered confiscation, social equality,
> high office and other inducements. Their place, most
> likely, in such a party would have been a lowly one and their
> direct power small. But, on the other hand, their right to
> vote would have probably been established.[31]

What a help this would have been to the Negro!

The fact is that the Negro, contrary to the claims of some critics, was not so enamored of his old pre-war status. And once he began to take his newly won freedom seriously, once he attempted to participate in some of the rights which went, theoretically, with the position he occupied as a free man, he became a real problem--a dangerous force. Once he refused to support the reactionary Bourbons, the Negro became a "threat to the supremacy of the white race." And the counter-revolutionary whites began seriously to study plans to remove the threat.

Incensed at the Republican victory in calling a convention and electing delegates thereto, the press began a bitter attack on the Negroes, who "have drawn a deep red blood line between themselves and the whites"[32] and with whom "principles are nothing and color everything."[33] The Enquirer defiantly declared "in the name of the white man not only of Virginia, but of the North, that the Negro shall not rule in this fair state designed by

God to be the dominion of the highest type of the white race. We unfurl the

standard of resistance to the wretched creatures who are soon to meet to

complete the work of Africanizing Virginia, and tell them that there are no

chains which they can forge in the shape of a mongrel organic law which can

bind the giant limbs of the Old Dominion."[34]

Hundreds of Negroes lost their jobs because they voted the Republican

ticket.[35] A newspaper in Lynchburg expressed its gratification that "one

hundred and fifty negroes employed at the Wythe Iron Mines, all of whom

voted the straight out radical ticket, were discharged on Tuesday by the

owner of the works.[36] Other papers expressed the opinion that henceforth

white laborers should be imported from the North and Europe.[37] They were

agreed that they must crowd the Negro out.

White chauvinism was rampant and the struggle was on. The call went

out for the holding of a "white man's convention" to organize the reaction-

ary forces. And on December 12, 1867, the leaders of the Old Democratic and

Whig parties assembled at Richmond.[38] A "white man's party" was created

and dedicated to the principle that "suffrage should be so regulated by the

States as to continue the Federal and State systems under the control and

direction of the white race."[39]

Alexander H. H. Stuart, outstanding aristocratic leader and president

of the reactionary convention, declared in his inaugural address:

> ...we will never submit to the rule of an alien race. We
> prefer the rule of the bayonet.... We desire further to
> protect our organization so that all who desire that this
> shall continue to be a white man's government may be able
> to act in concert and by a vigorous and united effort save
> ourselves from ruin and disgrace.[40]

The color line was now drawn, and the issue, on a racial basis had been definitely defined.[41] The Conservative party was "now organized," as Morton puts it, "to meet the new situation."[42]

The local press began a heated campaign to encourage white immigrants to come to Virginia for the purpose of displacing Negro labor. The Whig of October 28, 1867, "joyously" announced that another party of English immigrants had arrived in the state. The paper stated that:

> Our pleasure does not grow out of the fact that they are Englishmen but that they are white... We should welcome with outstretched arms every white man who comes amongst us, and treat him as a neighbor, a friend, and a brother.... The Negroes have chosen to draw the line between the two races and we must hail every white man....[43]

It was succinctly stated in conclusion that "We need their /white/ labor and we need them for political and social reasons."[44]

CHAPTER IV

THE CRISIS OF 1869 AND THE BEGINNING OF DISFRANCHISEMENT

The duly authorized constitutional convention met at Richmond, December 3, 1867, and proceeded to draw up a new organic law for Virginia.[1] This Assembly was dominated by white liberals, native and outsiders, with the voting power of the twenty-five Negroes offering decisive support. Some of the Negroes, like Dr. Thomas Bayne, of Norfolk,[2] were intelligent and fully cognizant of the problems and issues that faced the convention. The aristocratic elements were at a disadvantage because their most able spokesmen had been put under political disabilities as a result of their active participation in the rebellion.

Amid the sarcastic jibes and propaganda of an enraged local press, the convention began the task of bringing Virginia's fundamental law into keeping with the conditions of a new situation. Difficult problems of taxation, local government, education, civil rights, suffrage,[3] etc., were tackled and disposed of in commendable manner.[4] And after four eventful months, in which the recalcitrant white delegates had made repeated attempts to sabotage the liberal program, the convention, on April 17, 1868, brought its work to a close.

The new Constitution proposed a definite liberalization and democratization of the Old Dominion's legal, political and social institutions. It offered, or made possible, if accepted a real improvement over ante-bellum conditions. This instrument, derisively called the "Underwood Constitution," after Judge John C. Underwood, the presiding officer, provided for equal and uniform taxation on different kinds of property.[5] A uniform and equitable tax policy was a badly needed reform as the aristocratic regime had always shifted a disproportionate share of the tax burden to those least able to bear it.[6] The old method of voting viva voce, which often resulted in corruption, was abolished and the more democratic secret ballot introduced. This measure was vigorously opposed by the reactionaries, who realized its value in fighting machine politics, but it was subsequently adopted throughout the country.

The constitution proposed to renovate Virginia's backward and out-moded educational structure by authorizing a system of free public schools.[7] The Negroes in the convention had insisted on the establishment of a more democratic educational system. Although admitting that this provision for educational improvement was "a blessing", Morton concludes, as had the reactionaries in the convention, that it "was a great financial burden at that time and was not cordially received by many." This program would make possible, for the first time, mental instruction for the 70,000 illiterate whites of the state as well as the Negroes.[8]

The constitution guaranteed civil equality to black and white alike. All men, 21 years of age, without distinction of color, could vote, hold office and sit on juries--provided, of course, that they were sane and had not committed certain crimes.[9] The suffrage article also contained a disfranchising section which proposed to bar those who had participated in, or aided, the cause of the rebellion. It was further stipulated that all State, county, and city officers be required to take an oath that they had not borne arms against the United States and were not disqualified by the provisions of the new constitution.[10]

The convention had specified that the constitution be submitted to the approval of the people on the second of the following June, but several

things transpired to prevent this. The white leaders were bitterly opposed
to the proposed constitution because of the disfranchising clauses and the
"iron-clad" oath. The section granting the Negro equal civil and political
rights also drew the condemnation of many whites. They, therefore,
instituted a movement to defeat the brain child of the "mongrel convention."[11]
The Conservatives called upon General Schofield to delay submitting the
constitution to the people. Being hostile to the instrument the General
refused to call the proposed elections, on the grounds that he had not been
authorized to take the money necessary for holding the elections from the
treasury.[12] This was a mere sham since, as military commander, he had the
right, and indeed, it was expected that, in carrying out Congressional
instruction, he would provide for elections to determine the attitude of the
people on the issue.

General Schofield, however, went over to the side of reaction and
advised Congress to void the work of the convention.[13] In the meantime, the
Conservative leaders were stirring up sentiment against the constitution
throughout the State. At first the opposition had come mainly from the
press and the old leaders. The latter were clearly aware that if the public
accepted the constitution with the franchise and test oath provisions
their political future and the security of the interests they represented
would be in danger. Their control had lasted for so long that they had
developed a vested interest in political office. Again, the hitherto secure
ascendancy of the aristocratic class had been checked and, from some indica-
tions, might be impossible of reestablishment in the future. Thus it was
necessary that the constitution be defeated at all costs.

The old leaders found that opposition to the proposed constitution
was not by any means as strong among the middle and lower class whites as

they had hoped and claimed.[14] The aristocrats saw in the silence of these elements a realization on the part of the latter that the newly created organic law was desirable, and that the interests of the lower classes would be better served by its adoption. The reactionaries, therefore, finding no great indigenous antagonism to the constitution, decided to concentrate their attack on the test oath and disfranchising clause. They knew that if they could secure their freedom of action by having their political disabilities removed they would be in a much more advantageous position. Accordingly, a delegation was formed to go to Washington to put their case before Congress.[15] A "Committee of Nine" of the most "outstanding leaders" left for the National Capital to "acquaint Congress with the true state of affairs in Virginia and to save the State from the evils that impended."[16]

This action was the culmination of what has been called the "new movement" in Virginia.[17] As a concession to the Radicals in Congress, the leaders of this movement declared that they had forgone their opposition to Negro suffrage. They claimed that they had no objection to the Negro being given the vote. Cleverly, they selected as their motto, "unrestricted suffrage" and "universal amnesty."[18] They thus hoped that by linking these two measures the latter might be obtained as the price of submission to the former. And pleading their willingness to "surrender their opposition to" the Negro voter, they urged that the State be returned to the Union" on the basis of universal suffrage and universal amnesty."[19] The National Intelligencer (A District of Columbia news sheet) noting that the "Former ruling class of Virginia has steadfastly opposed negro suffrage...", stated that their leaders had bowed to the recent elections and now seek "impartial suffrage and universal amnesty...."[20] Continuing, the paper charged that "Since their defeat the attitude of these men has seemed sullen and discontented, if not dangerous. They come now bearing the olive branch."[21] The article was concluded with the statement that the Negroes of Virginia regarded the "new movement" as "a new device of the old enemy, whom they hold it a test of loyalty to fight forever and forever."[22]

The pleas of these men were quite successful and, after a struggle between the friends and opponents of radical reconstruction, they received favorable reactions from the Reconstruction Committee and President-elect Grant. Definitive action, however, was not had until April 1869, at which time Congress authorized President Grant to hold the election in Virginia and that, as he had recommended, certain parts of the constitution should be submitted separately.[23]

A few weeks later the President set July 6, 1869, as the date of election, specifying that separate votes be taken on the disfranchisement clause and test oath.[24]

This victory by the reaction was aided by the fact that the Republican delegations which went before the Reconstruction Committee were split into two bitterly opposed factions. Two Republican committees had gone to Washington from Virginia to testify on the issue of the constitution. One of these committees,[25] convinced that the future of the Republican Party in Virginia was at stake, urged that the Constitution, with the disfranchising clause and test oath, be submitted together. The committee expressed the belief that if the State came under reactionary control the Negroes and loyal whites would come in for intense intimidation. However, the other Republican committee, representing a growing conservative wing within the party, advocated that the test oath and section on disfranchising the ex-Confederates be submitted separately. This group was adverse to putting the native white element under any political disabilities and did not feel that the party should champion equality of rights for the Negro.

Having secured their demands, the Conservatives returned to
Virginia and immediately began plans for the coming election, at which, in
addition to the vote on the constitution, members of the State Legislature
were to be elected. In the convention, called by the Conservatives for the
purpose of nominating their candidates, it was stated in a minority report that

> .... the military rule of one of our race responsible to
> his superiors, is far preferable to the negroes; and that,
> impelled by these considerations we call upon all white
> men whether native or adopted citizens to vote down the
> constitution, and thereby save themselves and their
> posterity from negro suffrage, negro office-holding, and
> its legitimate consequence--negro social equality.[26]

Their speakers toured the State[27] and emphasized to their listeners the
necessity of defeating the objectionable parts of the constitution and
electing a Conservative ticket. Considerable effort was exerted to secure
the support of the Negroes. They were told that the Conservatives were
their best friends and that they owed it to themselves as well as Virginia
to vote against the Republicans. It was charged that there was a serious
split in Republican ranks and thus it was futile to vote that ticket.[28] It
was said that Wells, in subsequently declaring against the disfranchising
and test-oath sections of the Constitution, had sold-out the Negroes.[29] A
number of Negroes went over to the Conservatives and organized several
clubs in support of Conservative candidates.[30]

In some sections where there was a heavy black population, the
whites had more than one Negro nominated for certain offices and thus
divided the Negro vote. This enabled the white candidate, backed up by a
minority but solid white vote, to win the election. Some of the Negroes
nominated by whites were victorious.[31] As in the election on the convention
issue in 1867, Negroes were threatened with the loss of their jobs if they
voted Republican. Because of the comfortable majority of white voters in

Virginia, it was unnecessary to resort to the widespread coercive tactics which were coming into vogue in the states further South.[32]

In the campaign among the Negroes, the Union League was very active. This secret organization, devoted to developing the political intelligence of the freedmen, did much to solidify the Negro in Republican ranks.[33] The League held numerous secret meetings, usually at night, in which the rights and duties of citizenship, as well as the intricacies of politics, were explained to men only a few years removed from slavery. This crusading body, directed for the most part by ardent partisans from the North, was of great help to the Negroes who had had little experience in the political affairs of the state. It frequently prevented them from being victimized by the skilled whites. While acting extensively and importantly in Virginia politics of the latter sixties, this revolutionary instrument, forged in the bourgeois attempt to consolidate the gains won on the battle-field, did not rise to the heights it attained in South Carolina, where its role was more vital.[34] Before it went to pieces, after 1870, however, the League had wielded considerable influence in the affairs of Virginia, as the bitter hostility of the whites will testify.[35]

After a hectic campaign the people on July 6, 1869 went to the polls to accept or reject the constitution, and the separate clauses, and to elect members of the Legislature. After a tense day of voting, it was announced that the Conservative ticket had been elected. The official results, however, were not announced until the 9th of the following September.[36] The vote for Walker, the Conservative nominee, was 119,535 to 101,204 for Wells, the Republican. Dr. Harris, the Negro candidate for Lieutenant Governor on the Republican ticket, polled 99,600 to 120,068 for his opponent.[37] The constitution was ratified by the overwhelming vote of

206,233, only 9,189 votes being cast against it.[38] The disfranchising clause and the test oath were defeated by 124,361 to 84,404 for the former, and 124,106 to 83,114 for the latter.[39] Completing their day of victory, the reactionaries gained a decisive majority in both houses of the General Assembly. Only 13 out of 43 State Senators were Republicans. Six Negroes, three of whom were Conservatives, w ere elected to the upper house.[40] In all, 21 Negroes were sent to the legislature.[41] Out of a total of 138 delegates elected, 93 were Conservatives. The reactionaries had won a complete victory. The State was firmly in their control, as were 5 of the 9 Congressional districts.

The victory was noisly celebrated in reactionary circles. It was jubilantly announced that the Old Dominion had been "restored".[42] Throughout the State, the newspapers proclaimed that Virginia had been "redeemed, regenerated and disenthralled."[43] The Lynchburg press stated that the "deluded Negroes have been taught a lesson which will bring them to their senses," and was confident that from then on "we will have no more trouble with them."[44] In a more subdued and constructive tone the Danville Register, now that reactionary control stood achieved, was moved to suggest that the vanquished forget their loss and that "all of us now go to work, white and colored, looking forward hopefully to a just and liberal system of legislation and on impartial administration for the protection of all alike."[45] A Richmond newspaper thanked "our colored allies" who "are brave and true men, who deserve our respect, confidence, and affection."[46]

The apprehension of the Negroes, however, was not so easily allayed. They could not understand why the black vote should shrink from 105,832 to 97,105.[47] The white vote had increased from the 1867 total of 120,101 to 125,114. The Negro vote, contrary to what could have been normally expected,

had fallen off by 8,600 votes. Under ordinary circumstances it would seem
that the Negro vote should have been greater, rather than smaller, in this
election which came two years after the first registration and after a long,
heated campaign. At this time the Negro, in the flush of his newly found
rights, was eagerly and enthusiastically using them as a test as well as an
expression of liberty. He had none of the apathy, born of opposition and
disillusionment, that was to come later. Typical of their anxious anticipa-
tion was the incident at Alexandria when, only three days after passage of
the first Reconstruction Act, they had surged to the polls and attempted
to vote.[48]

Incensed at the Conservative victory, the Republicans protested that
"the election held in this State on the 6th day of July, last, resulted in
a Confederate triumph, which we unhesitatingly assert was achieved by
artifice, intimidation and fraud."[49] A few weeks later black and white
Republicans, assembled in a convention called for the purpose of reorganizing
the party, declared that

> Threats of violence prevented the exercise of free discussion
> during the campaign.... In some instances our meetings were
> broken up by mobs, the leaders of which have as yet gone
> unpunished.[50]

They also charged that Negroes, "dependent upon their labors for support,
were threatened with loss of labor"; and that "a war of extermination, even,
was not infrequently held out before them in case they voted for the
separate clauses and the Republican ticket."[51] The convention was aware that
the "General Assembly... is controlled by a majority who have constantly
denounced its liberal provisions," and doubted, therefore, "that the
constitution would be carried out in full faith, unless Congress can exact
guarantees...."[52] The Convention urged that Congress either "require the

test oath of officers elected, or a new election on the Constitution as a whole.[53]

Notwithstanding this urgent representation, the national administration was not moved and President Grant, ignoring the requests, on December 6, 1869, recommended to Congress that Virginia be speedily readmitted to the Union. The President, on January 26, signed the Congressional act which accepted Virginia's representatives.[54] The next day the military commander turned the state over to the civil authorities.[55] The General Assembly convened in October and on the eighth of that month the 14th and 15th Amendments were ratified, the former by a vote of 36 to 4 in the Senate and 126 to 6 in the House of Delegates, and the latter by 40 to 2 in the upper, and unanimously in the lower chambers.[56]

The forces of reaction were triumphant. The old leadership was firmly back in power. And although they had found it necessary to make some concessions, the only basic difference was that now there was a broader base or source of power, brought on by the enlargement of the electorate, and thus requiring greater effort and political ingenuity to hold in line. But whatever the future held, Virginia had been "restored" to the people.

CHAPTER V

THE BEGINNING OF "LEGAL" ELIMINATION

Although the Conservatives had come into almost complete control
of the political machinery of the State, they did not hesitate in further
consolidating their gains and insuring their continuous domination. This
activity was divided into two tactical approaches: first, propaganda,
especially through the channels of the local press, was effectively
utilized to foster the development of favorable public opinion towards the
Conservative administration -- thus securing white support at the polls; the
second tactic consisted of trying to obtain the Negro vote, and, failing this,
to nullify it. In keeping with the first tactic, one tabloid stated on
July 12, 1870, that the recently adjourned legislature "... did a great deal
of work. We have never known a more industrious legislative body."[1] Continuing, the paper said that although "compelled to put into operation a
Constitution which is so awkwardly and ambiguously worded that no one can
say with certainty what many of its provisions mean," the "members have
done credit to themselves."[2] Referring to the Negroes in the Assembly, the
same editor wrote of the subsequent legislative session that although"...
there was a new element in the body during the session just past, which
occasioned embarrassment and perplexity," the results were "remarkably
successful ... and its devotion to the public interest has been clearly
proved."[3] This was another of the methods used to discredit the Negro's
political ability and bias opinion against his participation in the franchise.

The efforts of the Conservatives to solidify their supremacy were
constantly successful. Their many-pointed attack on the political position

of the Negro made steady progress. Each subsequent election witnessed the utilization of racial antipathy as a means of effecting the victory of Conservative candidates. In the campaign of 1871 the number of Negro delegates in the Assembly was reduced from 23 to 14, and in the Senate from 6 to 3.[4] The Conservatives made the "race question" the main point of emphasis in the election of 1873. The presence of the Negro in the Legislature was used to illustrate the possibility of "negro domination." Calling upon all whites to "be true to their race by supporting their party",[5] the reactionaries went so far as to accuse all Negro men of being ever-willing and anxious to rape the South's "fair white womanhood." In this mood the Lynchburg Republican editorialized: "It seems monstrous to suppose that any white man, having a mother, sister, wife, or daughter, can march up to the polls and vote to place in power a party which connives at such outrages."[6] Referring to the strife then taking place in the lower States,[7] the demagogues demanded that the whites of the state join in a solid white front and "save Virginia." "And the horrible example," as one writer in a doctoral thesis, puts it, "of Radical-negro rule that could then be seen in other Southern states afforded the white Conservatives an ample and just reason for the existence of their party."[8]

So effective was this appeal to the emotions that many "of the ignorant native whites believed that they were in danger of being ruled by their former slaves."[9] The returns of the election showed a Conservative victory by a comfortable margin. This frequent intensification and utilization of racial antagonism as an instrument for guaranteeing the continuity of Conservative control was undoubtedly due, in great part, to a growing unrest among the lower stratum of southern society and the necessity of guarding against any threat of revolt in Conservative ranks.

The State was undergoing a period of great difficulty. Economic reconstruction was slowly and painfully taking place.[10] In 1873 the panic and depression which struck the country made considerable impression in the Old Dominion. It was necessary, therefore, to have an effective weapon with which to counteract any growth of indigenous opposition in white ranks.

Naturally this description of the Negro as an irresponsible and dangerous force, not deserving of any political privileges, was bound to cause a reaction in the black electorate. It served to further strengthen the hold of Republicanism on the Negro voter and gave increased pertinency to Fred Douglass' classic allusion to the Republican Party as "the ship and all else the sea."[11] Loyalty to the G. O. P. often led to the social ostracism of any Negro who voted the Conservative ticket. There were cases of Negro ministers (to whom the loyalty of the congregation was usually almost fanatical) having been forced to give up their churches because of political mistakes of this nature.[12] Religious congregations were not adverse to expelling a wayward member because of political disloyalty.[13] There were also many instances in which Negroes, having changed their political allegiance to conform to the desires of the whites, suffered severe physical harm from enraged fellow blacks.[14]

During this period the elimination of the Negro vote had usually been accomplished by general corruption, such as counting out ballots and vote manipulation and coercive practices. The ever increasing strength of Conservatism, however, led many of its partisans to advocate reenforcing the many methods of illegal exclusion with "legal" elimination. And since the majority of the Negroes evinced no great tendency to join Conservative ranks, a movement was launched to disfranchise as many of them as possible by means of the law.

The Gerrymander of Black Districts

The first step in this direction was taken in 1871 when the Conservatives, making use of their overwhelming majority in the Legislature, enacted a statute which re-defined the boundaries of many counties in such a way that Negro majorities were split up and so divided among the whites that they were nullified.[15] This gerrymandering neutralized a considerable portion of the Negro vote in the Black Belt,[16] the only section in which the colored electorate wielded a preponderance of power. The manipulation of county boundaries and the redistribution of representation in the interest of partisan politics was a relatively easy matter, for the constitution of 1869, in providing for a reapportionment of local representation after each census, had not specified what the basis of such reallocation should be. Thus the political machine was in a periodic position to make strategic redefinition of boundaries and representation in the interest of its domination. Chandler states that

> The whole power is in the hands of the Legislature, and thus opportunities are afforded for fraud. Any political party in power at the time of reapportionment has the power to adopt any basis for that reapportionment, and to gerrymander the State for party aggrandisement.[17]

This weapon was repeatedly used to Conservative advantage.[18]

Disfranchisement by Constitutional Amendment

Increasingly desirous of overcoming the superior numerical strength of the Negroes in the counties with black majorities, the Conservatives in 1873 proposed an amendment to the Constitution which would completely reorganize the system of county government. This amendment authorized the Legislature to cut down the number of State officials.[19] It was submitted to the people in 1874[20] and was successfully pushed through in the fall elections.[21] This measure was specifically aimed at taking the control of local government in the black districts out of the hands of the Negroes. Immediately after its passage a large number of colored officials were dropped, as "one-third of the local offices... were abolished."[22]

The Poll Tax Amendment

The Virginia Legislature of 1874-75 continued the attack on Negro suffrage by proposing two additional groups of amendments to the State constitution. The first group, relating to the franchise, proposed, first, to make the payment of the poll tax a requisite for voting.[23] The next General Assembly submitted to the people the proposed amendment requiring that, in order to vote, every elector, in addition to the requirements of age and residence, must "... have paid to the State, before the day of election, the capitation tax required by law, for the preceding year..."[24] Although directed at the Negro,[25] the urgent need for State revenue helped to secure support for this measure.

The Crime Amendment

The other amendment in the first group also related to the franchise. This amendment, proposed in 1874-75,[26] would add petit larceny to the list of crimes disqualifying their perpetrators from voting.[27] These two amendments, submitted and approved in 1876,[28] "were aimed directly at the negro for it was thought that many would fail to pay the tax, and petit larceny was a common offense among them."[29]

In addition it was proposed to strike from the constitution the section containing the following oath which had been required of persons offering to register:

> I, _____ _____, do solemnly swear (or affirm) that I
> am not disqualified from exercising the right of suffrage
> by the constitution framed by the convention which
> assembled in the city of Richmond, on the third of December,
> eighteen hundred and sixty-seven, and that I will support
> and defend the same to the best of my ability.[30]

The second group of amendments to the constitution dealt with the legislature. These amendments proposed that the number of delegates in the Assembly be cut to "not more than one hundred"[31] and that the Legislature meet biennially instead of annually as before.[32] Another significant amendment that was proposed provided that

> The legislature shall have power to provide for the govern-
> ment of cities and towns, and to establish such courts
> therein as may be necessary for the administration of
> justice.[33]

These several constitutional amendments were ratified in 1876,[34] in the usual manner of pressure politics and legislation enforcing them was approved April 2, 1877.[35]

Although they had been enthusiastically advocated by the reactionaries, these legislative methods of reducing the Negro vote did not yield the predicted results. As a matter of fact, neither one of the reasons for the institution of the capitation tax was served to any considerable extent. It "did not materially increase the amount of school revenue",[36] and neither did it form too much of an obstacle to the colored electors. In those days most Negroes set a high value on the ballot.[37] The right of indicating their political choices by dropping a little slip of paper into the poll boxes was regarded as an indispensable expression of liberty and their recently acquired status. Those interested enough paid their taxes[38] and others, provided they voted "sensibly," were not required to pay. Still others, if their vote was of real consequence, were registered by "political agents" who took care that the tax was paid in due time."[39]

Speaking of the general dissatisfaction resulting from the poll tax requirement, one writer states that there was no provision as to just when the tax should be paid--that is, no definite time limit was specified. Therefore, "It was consequently often paid at the last moment for the voter. Fraud resulted," and especially galling to the Conservatives, "much money was needed by each party for the purchase of votes."[40] Another objection to the poll tax requisite came from the poor whites. Particularly was this true in the mountanous regions of western Virginia where Republicanism was predominant among the white population. The whites of this section, finding the Conservatives effectively wielding the capitation tax as a weapon to disfranchise them,[41] added their voices to the opposition.

Discouragement and Decline of Power

The Conservatives, having gained control of the State in the first election, 1869, were rapidly consolidating their domination as time went on. They had "hamstrung" the Negro vote wherevever necessary and had discommoded any indigenous revolt that threatened in white Conservative ranks. The challenge "be true to your race" had served to solidify the white forces into an alignment devoid of class considerations. The ordinary corrupt methods of excluding the Negro had gone on apace and had been bulwarked by legislative and constitutional provisions for disfranchising him. His political progress was being so effectively hindered that the Negro was moved to call upon the national Republican administration and his friends of the North to succor him.

Gathered in convention at Richmond, August 20, 1875, the Negroes charged that they were suffering "at the hands not only of the white citizens and local government of Virginia, but also at the hands of the leaders of the Republican party within the State and in the Federal capital."[42]

The convention declared that "while we reiterate unflinching fidelity to the principles of the Republican party, and, per consequence, fealty to the Administration, we again respectfully ask and think it right for the Administration to stretch out its hand and save us and the organization as it exists..."[43]

The convention also expressed its

.... utmost anxiety and alarm at the condition of the disorganization and disaffection existing in the party in the State, caused by the appointment of a number of Federal officeholders all over the State, many instances of which occur to us who are pronounced Democrats, who would blush Judas-like were Republican sentiments imputed to them, and of others who are an incubus to the party and are preparing the way for a precipitate desertion into the Democratic lines in case the late lamented Confederacy shall succeed in establishing its power and supremacy again in 1876.[44]

Frequent controversies between white and colored Republican leaders and between leadership and followers had occurred. Some of the colored voters were of the opinion that the white Republican leaders were more interested in securing office for themselves than rights for the Negro.[45] The acceptance of this view was greatly facilitated by the constant attempts of the Conservatives to alienate the Negro from white Republican leadership.[46] Feuds between prominent white and colored Republicans over nominations and other points had done much to intensify discord in the party. The situation was further confused by an internal split of the party into "radical," or liberal and "conservative" wings.[47] The unqualified advocacy of Negro equality was often the dividing line between these two groups.

However, the Negroes were to find that they could expect little aid from their northern friends, whose attention was diverted to more urgent conditions nearer home. The national economic depression of 1873,[48] the nation-wide march away from Republican ranks in 1874 and other vital considerations, kept the North well occupied.[49] The South was thus left

to seek its "salvation" as it so saw fit. Virginia, along with the other

restored states, was free to deal with the Negro and the franchise in

any manner she cared to. In 1872 Congress removed the political

disabilities imposed on the old leaders by the 14th Amendment.[50] The cause

of the Negro thus received another set back.

By 1878, therefore, the Negro in Virginia, attacked at home and

snubbed nationally, found himself reduced to a position of negligible

importance in the political affairs of the State. Only in the Black Belt

did he still constitute a factor of any influence, and the legislative

and constitutional provisions were rapidly reducing his power there. So

well, indeed, was the black vote being nullified, that the Conservatives

were beginning to believe that their job was about finished. The Negro

thus faced this discouraging situation when the Readjusters came upon the

political scene in 1879, at which time almost the entire complexion of

things seemed destined to rapidly change.

CHAPTER VI

"READJUSTERISM" AND REACTION

The Readjuster movement, which catapulted the Negro into a position
of political importance again, developed out of the controversy surrounding
the State debt situation.[1] At first it had been primarily an issue within
the Conservative Party, but soon grew into an independent organization
embracing several elements. The issue arose as a result of differences of
opinion as to the handling of the pressing economic problems of the State.
Virginia found hereslf obligated to pay a huge public debt, a great part
of which had been incurred during the last years of the slave regime. The
Conservatives split over a choice of methods of dealing with payment of the
debt. One group, composed primarily of the aristocrats and wealthy classes,
advocated that the entire indebtedness, without change or reduction, be
paid.[2] This group became known as the "Funders."[3] The upper classes advocated the unconditional payment of the debt because they, the aristocracy
and the "city capitalistic interests",[4] constituted the largest local group
of bondholders. Secondly, the aristocracy was bitterly opposed to any considerable state support for education. They had prevented the improvement
and democratization of the school system because of the "levelling" effect
it would have on the class structure. When, as a result of financial
difficulties, it became necessary to choose between payment of the debt and
providing outlays for education, they were unqualifiedly for the latter.
These reactionaries regarded payment of the debt as a binding "moral
obligation" and looked upon education for the masses as an unnecessary
"luxury".[5] Further, a

prominent debt payer is said to have publicly stated that

it would be better to burn the school houses than to permit
the state to default in interest payment on the debt.[6]

Another group of Conservatives were of the opinion that the state's
creditors should be compelled to stand a part of the general loss occasioned
by the depression and war. This element, embracing for the most part, the
lower and underprivileged classes, was becoming increasingly hostile to the
privileged "bondholders," "brokers," and officeholding "rings."[7] They did not
desire that the State debt be completely repudiated, but insisted that it
should be "readjusted" so as to ease the already heavy tax burden.[8]

The leader of the Readjuster wing was General William Mahone, who
had failed by a narrow margin to win the Conservative nomination for governor
in the convention of 1877.[9] Although it has been charged that Mahone
"seized upon the idea of readjustment as the means of bringing himself into
power,"[10] the fact is that he simply made use of a real conflict of interest
in the party and identified himself with the group destined to win out. He
was a clever politician and a recognized strategist. In keeping with the
best American political tradition, he effectively utilized a highly contro-
versial issue. Moreover, the issue, in contrast to most political conflicts,
was basic and affected the majority of the people in one way or another.

The Readjuster element split from the Conservative standards in
1879 and went to the polls on an independent Readjuster ticket.[11] This
schism in Conservative ranks made the Negro vote a decided asset. Therefore
both the Funders and Readjusters went after the colored electors. The
poorer classes of citizens tended to support Mahone's party and the Negroes
were no exception. Their interest, they felt, would be doubly served by
aligning themselves against the Funders; first, they would be opposing an
increase in the tax burden, and second, they would be contributing to the
downfall of those who had dealt so harshly with their basic rights. On the

other hand the Readjusters offered them greater equality, political office and other desirable gains. Realizing the strategic importance of their support, the Negroes voted for Readjusterism.[12]

The Readjuster ticket was elected and it was clearly apparent that the defeat of the Funders was due to the colored vote.[13] The Negro had thus come to exercise a balance of power[14] in local politics and the whites faced the necessity of competing for the black ballot.

> Thus old issues were raised, negro Republicans were elected on the Readjuster ticket and voted for the Funder ticket,[15] and the negro had emerged again as a factor to be reckoned with in the politics of the State.[16]

Reaction to this new situation was immediate. Calling the reactionary-dominated press into service, it was charged that the "repudiators" as the Readjusters were called, had been put into office by Negro Republicans whose support had been gained despite "what Fred Douglass, President Hayes, and others of their party high in authority told them."[17] To further create racial antagonism and resentment against the Negro, it was claimed that the colored electors had "voted for a ticket that scarcely one reputable white Republican in this city could or would support."[18]

At first Readjuster leaders were not inclined to openly admit their alliance with the black voter, but on seeing their ranks steadily increased by both white and colored, they made "no bones" of the situation.[19] While the Negro constituted a chief source of Readjuster support, the fact was that a considerable number of the rank and file whites, whose very presence in the Conservative Party was an anomoly, had deserted to the Readjusters. It was also true that many white Republicans, some out of mere opposition to the reactionaries, were attracted to this party.[20] With the aid of these various elements, the Readjusters gained control of the General

Assembly in the election of 1879, and elected the governor two years later.[21] In traditional American manner, the victors received the "spoils" of war. And in the dispensation of political patronage, it was natural that the Negro should receive a reward for his services. Consequently, many offices were turned over to colored men,[22] particularly in the counties of the Black Belt.[23] And although these were minor positions for the most part, they represented a decided improvement over past conditions.

The appointment of Negroes to office only served to intensify the hatred of the reactionaries against them. They saw jobs that had been securely theirs for many years now occupied by "vicious and disreputable" elements.[24] Cognizant of the fact that the colored voter was the strongest link in a chain whose weak point was racial differences--ephemeral but no less real--a vicious assault was made upon this unit of the party. Stating that the Negroes had never manifested such an interest in politics as they had during the campaigns of 1879 and 1881, complaint was made that "we have to some extent been deceived again as to what the negroes would do."[25] One editor, after pointing out the tremendous Readjuster support among the colored electorate, argued that "It ought to be enough for the white men of Virginia to know that even a majority of the votes which defeated them were cast by negroes."[26]

In spite of the fact that the reactionaries denounced the Readjuster victory as "A Republican triumph"[27] and thus a triumph of Negroes whose "sole aim" was to vote against the local whites[28]-- it is clear that this new phenomena was far more than this. Essentially, Readjusterism was a class movement. It represented the protest of indigenous democratic forces against distressing conditions and continued Conservative domination. This movement cut sharply across racial lines and assumed the more fundamental aspects of a realistic political alignment, having as its raison d'etre economic interest. Virginia, for the first time since the Civil War, was experiencing effective class political organization and collaboration, as the forces of democracy, unleashed by the War and its aftermath, vigorously asserted themselves. The middle classes, small farmers, and Negroes, were for the most part, united in opposition to the "Bourbon Aristocrats."

It is obvious that the Negro, in aligning himself with, and becoming a part of, such a movement, was serving both his needs and the needs of the times. As an essentially working class group, at the very bottom of the underprivileged, he was a peculiar victim of Conservative domination and stood to gain much by its defeat. The colored electorate had usually faced resentment and intimidation in the attempted exercise of rights bestowed and, supposedly, guaranteed by the United States Constitution.[29] Their aspiration for political privileges and political office in keeping with their political responsibility had been rudely shattered. In spite of the provision in the State's organic law for a liberal public education system, the Negro child was still the victim of inequitable school facilities.[30] Again, Negro teachers, because of a wage differential, were poorly paid, and payment was quite irregular in some instances.[31]

The whipping post was still being "barbarously used by the Bourbons to degrade and disfranchise the colored people...."[32] And the ball and chain could be legally used on Negroes in the course of forced labor.[33] Though regularly, and often undeservedly the subject of court procedure and criminal prosecution, the Negro was barred from serving on juries.[34] All this, in addition to the general economic depression, made the position of the Negro distressing indeed. And it was the idea of alleviating these conditions that constituted the basic motivation behind Negro support for the

Readjusters.

"Readjusterism", well aware of the task before it, proceeded to fulfill its purposes. In addition to satisfactorily adjusting the debt downward, other liberal measures were enacted. An Amendment repealing the one which had made the payment of the capitation tax a requisite for voting was proposed[35] and, upon submission to the people[36] in the election of 1862, was ratified by a vote of 107,303 to 66,131.[37] One editor estimated that the abolition of the poll tax requirement would "add at least forty thousand to our voting strength."[38] Dissatisfaction among the whites with the Conservative program is indicated by an editorial in which a newspaper expressed the hope that

> This will be the last election in Virginia in which the use of money will be an absolute necessity.... The requirement of the capitation tax as a prerequisite for voting has been the source of all our ills and yet when it was adopted we were assured by the wise men who were the fathers of the movement that it was the only thing needed to make our elections pure and keep the government in the control of the best people.... The party in power /Conservatives/ had tax receipts ready made out in blank and signed by the collectors to be filled out up by the name of anyone offering it as a substitute or an original voter to cast his vote in the interest of the Boss....[39]

The tax rate on general property was reduced by the Readjuster legislature, and new schedules designed to ease the burden of the poor were prepared.[40] Business came in for greater regulation,[41] and, in shifting a more just share of public taxes to the wealthy interests, payment of long-overdue state claims against the railroads was pressed.[42] Labor conditions were improved--a "Labor Association of Lynchburg" being chartered. The whipping post was abolished. The school system received generous aid from the Readjusters. Since there was not a single institution of higher education for Negroes in the State, $100,000, and a specified yearly appropriation was devoted to the establishment of such an institution.[43] The _facts_ would indicate, therefore, that the Negro knew what he was doing when he joined in this democratic movement.

Almost everything the Readjusters did was criticized by the opposition leaders. These reactionaries were even opposed to the modernization of what had been called Virginia's "pauper school system," a name which "expressed the fundamental idea of the ruling class that a man's children should be educated by himself, in proportion to his social status."[44] Pearson further states that

> Any considerable education of the masses, they believed, must lead to unrest which would result in disappointment or in "levelling."[45]

It was only logical, then, that the forces of reaction were opposed to Readjusterism in all its manifestations. The "Bourbons" were thoroughly frightened by the revolt and speedy rise to power of this "poor man's party." The old leaders were anxious to reestablish their former oligarchic dominance and quickly began to gird themselves for a battle to destroy this new political phenomenon. As "Readjusterism" was an embodiment of the needs and aspirations of an economic class, it was realized that this sphere offered no encouraging possibilities for the opposition. Thus the Conservative leaders turned to the weakest point in the unity of their opponents—the race "issue"—the instrument that had been so successfully utilized in the building of that political anomaly and monstrosity—the "Solid South." Gathering their shattered forces, the Conservatives met in convention in Lynchburg on July 1883, and welded all anti-Mahonites into a new "white man's party." This organization was dedicated to the defeat of "Mahoneism" and although a new name was assumed—the "Democrats"[46]—it was composed of the same old reactionary elements. "Mahoneism," the object at which the assault was directed,[47] was a mere smoke screen for the aspiring politicians.

In the following election campaign of 1883 the race issue received unprecedented emphasis. The Negro was assailed as being ignorant, unscrupulous and devoid of any vestiges of civilized characteristics. Charges of rape were often brought into play. One speaker, at the height of a vitriolic outburst, informed his listeners that "I am a Democrat because I am a white man and a Virginian."[48] In their determination to win, the reactionaries abandoned "every issue except the false one of color...." and subordinated everything to "... the exploiting of the negro as a scare crow...."[49] As the struggle progressed it was charged that John S. Barbour, State Chairman of the Conservative Party, "created a dictatorship...to reinforce fraud with violence," so that "victory for Bourbonism" could be "achieved at all hazzards and all costs."[50]

In the past the Democrats had not found it necessary to resort to actual violence on a large scale as they had controlled the election machinery. But now that their partisans could not manipulate the votes as of yore, they engaged extensively in overt intimidation. Bloody conflict flared in scattered sections of the State. In a highly tense atmosphere at Danville, Virginia, a riot occurred in which several persons were killed.[51] It has been alleged that the fracas resulted from the "accidental discharge of a pistol during a dispute between a white man and two negroes."[52] But as charged,[53] it would seem that the entire affair was deliberately planned and perpetrated for the purpose of arousing sentiment against the Negro, solidifying white support for the Democrats and frightening the colored voters away from the polls. In substantiation of this view, it is significant that immediately after the riot there followed "a false and heroic call to arms for defense against the negroes who (with thousands of white Republicans) were cowering in terror or flying in panic from the execution of a plot which Virginia Bourbons had learned to form from the examples given in South, Carolina, Alabama...."[54]

The day following the "Danville massacre", which was the day before election, the following telegram was sent to all parts of the Southwest: "We are standing in our doors, with shot guns in hand, defending our wives and children from an organized mob of negroes now parading the streets!" The real situation seems to have been that "a colored man was not to be seen in the streets of Danville on that day."[55] On the contrary, "an armed force of white men was parading the streets on that very day."[56] Nevertheless, the incident intensified race feeling throughout the State and racial contact became fraught with danger. Rabble-rousers declared that "no negro is fit to make laws for white people."[57] Indeed, the Conservatives "hoisted both the black flag and the bloody shirt..."[58]

On the day of election almost every known method of corruption was resorted to by the "Bourbon-Barbourite-Democracy".[59] Counting out and re-marking of votes, the use of tissue ballots, and other means were utilized to eliminate the Negro. This comprehensive assault on Readjuster unity was overwhelming. The common front of these economically consistent elements, already unstable by virtue of the historical racial antipathy created and implanted by the slave regime, was shattered. The "threat" of Virginia's being "Africanized"[60] was too great for the whites of the State.[61] The returns of the election of 1883 showed a Republican rout.[62] The Democrats elected a majority in both houses of the legislature.[63]

The campaign had revolved around race and on this basis the contest had been decided. In this light it is clear that with economic issues being totally obscured by the bogey of race, "The alliance with the blacks,

which was the chief element of Mahone's strength, proved, in the end, to be
his undoing."[64] Efforts to construct an intelligible political alignment
in the State had been frustrated. Class politics, long and badly needed,
was aborted by the reactionary leaders and their rabble-rousing henchmen.
Naturally, the Negro, along with his supposedly victorious white brothers,
had lost much by this turn of events. The resulting reaction effectively
augmented the movement to bring about the political impotency of the Negro.
As McDaniel says, the action of

> Mahone and his followers to secure the dominance of their
> party taught the Democrats how to exclude the Negro from
> participation in politics. Mahone had resurrected the
> spectre of negro domination, of "Africanization" and there-
> after the white people of the Black Belt regarded as
> excusable any means that would assure white supremacy.[65]

By the time the new legislature convened the Democrats had evolved
a plan by which the election machinery was to be "renovated" in keeping with
changed conditions. The reactionaries desired to create a self-perpetuating
machine in order to insure the perpetuity of Democratic control. Therefore
the Assembly of 1883-84 had as a major item on its legislative calendar a
new election bill. This measure, as finally passed,[66] provided that the
legislatures have the power to appoint an electoral board "of three free-
holders" for each city and county. These Commissions were given authority
to appoint local officials to conduct elections.[67] The law did not require
that these free holders or the election officials be of different political
parties. This bill, passed over Cameron, the Readjuster incumbent's head,
was immediately voided by the Court of Appeals on the grounds that the act
imposed a free-hold qualification for office and thus violated Article IV
of the State constitution.[68]

The Democrats, however, were not to be stopped. They forced the

Governor to call a special session of the legislature, the purpose of which
was to afford them another opportunity "to take possession" of the ballots
and elections. At this extra session of 1884, the Democrats drew up a bill
which would serve their purpose without violating the State or Federal
Constitutions. This Act, known as the Anderson-McCormick law, was[69] again
passed over Governor Cameron's head. It contained substantially the same
provisions as its predecessor, with the exception that the section requiring
the members of the city and county electoral boards to be free-holders was
omitted. This omission insured the constitutionality of the law.[70]

The electoral boards set up by the Anderson-McCormick law were
selected by the Assembly,[71] and the election officials appointed by these
boards thus had to meet the approbation of the Democratic legislators. This
"Democratization" of Virginia's entire election machinery--the electoral
boards, registrars and judges--meant "the complete and perpetual mastery of
the people by Bourbonism."[72] Aware of this situation, the Richmond Times
charged that this change in the State's election law "was made for no other
reason than that the Democratic Party might control the electors in the
negro counties without regard to votes...." that the "Democratic party
might carry the negro counties by fraud and election tricks...."[73] To the
Times' denunciation of the new law as a bill "passed to encourage ballot-box
stuffing,"[74] The Richmond Dispatch replied frankly and unmistakably:

> The Anderson-McCormick bill was passed in the interest of
> the white people of Virginia.... It is a white man's law.
> It operates to perpetuate the rule of the white man.[75]

CHAPTER VII

DISFRANCHISEMENT BY FRAUD IS BULWARKED BY BRUTALITY

Finding themselves back in power, the Democrats immediately turned
to consolidating their gains. They were determined to erect sufficient
safeguards to prevent a return to power by their opponents. There followed
a wholesale dismissal of Readjusters from office, as the Democrats set about
building a powerful political machine.[1] This "purge" catapulted John
Mitchell, Jr., who was to become the most outstanding Negro in political and
business circles of the State, into the arena of politics. The Readjusters
had appointed several Negro principals in colored schools.[2] This action was
unprecedented as Virginia had formerly placed white men at the head of Negro
schools. Therefore, when the Democrats returned to power in 1883, a movement was immediately begun to oust the colored principals. The Planet,[3] a
local colored newspaper to which Mitchell often contributed articles, con-
demned the proposed dismissals in an outspoken editorial. Regarding this
action as another example of Negro "insolence", the new school board dismissed "a large number of the male Negro teachers, and John Mitchell was
one of these."[4] Mitchell soon became editor and manager of the Planet[5] and
subsequently developed into a dominant figure and militant race leader.

The governor had not come up for election in 1883 and thus a Readjuster still occupied that office. However, his power of appointment was
drastically curtailed,[6] and the Democratic legislature, steadily increasing
its control over appointments, consistently blocked any move of the executive to place his men in office. Remembering the important influence which
Negroes had frequently exercised in local government during the period of

Readjuster control, the Democrats adopted measures to change this situation and to prevent its recurrence. The charters of these towns containing large Negro majorities were amended[7] so as to prevent the Negroes from having any effective voice in governmental affairs.[8] The Legislature again resorted to gerrymandering, thereby reapportioning local and Congressional districts "in favor of the Democratic party."[9]

Each subsequent election saw a greater consolidation of reactionary control. The Democrats were in control of the election machinery and thus could and did wield it as an effective means of "handling" the Negro vote. The Richmond Times charged that the election set up was designed "for no other reason than that the Democratic party might control the elections in the negro counties without regard to votes."[10] Speaking of this southern practice, one authority says that "It was, indeed, through their exclusive and carefully maintained control of the voting and the count that the whites found the best opportunities for illegal methods."[11] The Democrats, therefore, found little difficulty in "counting out" unfavorable ballots.[12] In Mahone's desperate battles of 1884 and 1885, the Republicans[13] were crushed. After the defeat of his party in the latter year, General Mahone announced that

> The Democrats have carried the State legislative tickets by
> unscrupulous use of the election machinery, over which they
> have absolute control, which was provided by their past
> usurping legislature with this end in view.[14]

Many years later a local politician wrote that in the election of 1889, in which Mahone again ran for governor, "Thirty thousand votes were stricken from the registration books by Democratic orders just before the election, and the ticket of Mahone, Slemp and Lurtz lost the state by a large majority."[15]

Further Methods of Elimination

Democratic corruption grew by leaps and bounds and, with it, the steady elimination of the Negro. An extensively used method of reducing the colored vote in precincts where they constituted a majority was to delay the line of Negro electors.[16] Frequently so much time was taken in the voting that Negroes found it necessary to stand in line for several hours in order to cast their ballots. Many often became disgusted and left without getting near the booth.[17] It was not unusual to find, at the closing of the polls, long lines of colored electors waiting but unable to vote.

There were many ways of delaying the line of Negro voters. Much time was frequently consumed in finding the names of the colored electors on the registration books.[18] Again, before each Negro was permitted to cast his vote his name was checked against the list of persons who had been disfranchised as a result of a crime.[19] There were numerous men with the same names, and where that of a legitimate elector was similar to another on the registration list, he faced the necessity of proving his identity. While gathering material for this essay in Richmond, the writer was told of an instance in which the election officials transported a number of aged Civil War veterans to the polls in old Jackson Ward of that city and spent hours in voting them. During all this time the colored electors had to wait patiently in line. Needless to say, many left without casting their ballots.[20]

Nor did the black voter have much chance of securing redress from these tactics. They could and often did seek relief from this practice of closing the polls on lines of Negro electors. The Richmond Dispatch of October 31, 1888, carried an article stating that the county had heard several appeals that day from the decisions of election registrars and that "the cases were nearly all of colored voters who had failed to reach the

polls before sundown," at which time the polls were closed.[21] After hearing
the Negroes protest against not being allowed to cast their legal ballots,
the article continued, "All of this class were shut out by the Courts, both
Republicans and Democratic Judges deciding that they had no ground for
appeal."[22] Resort to the courts thus was usually of little avail to Negroes
who had been illegally kept from voting.

Still another ruse used to cut down the black vote was the practice
of election challengers embarrassing and delaying colored voters by asking
numerous and irrelevant questions. For example, a man of seventy, who had
lived in the precinct for twenty years, was asked "whether he lived in the
precinct, whether he was twenty-one years of age, when he became of age, when
he was born, where his parents reside, where they were born",[23] and so forth.
One of the most effective methods used to insure victory for the Democracy
was that of stuffing the ballot boxes. Democratic election officials became
quite expert at this practice.[24] The Richmond Times, a Democratic paper,
commenting on the corrupt election machinery, charged that in the "negro
districts the election officials do all the voting (or counting, which makes
it amount to the same thing)...."[25] An election official, in sworn testimony before the House Committee on Privileges and Elections, stated that

> at some of the voting places in my county and others adjoin-
> ing it, the ballot-boxes were placed in a remote part of the
> room out of view of the electors who were required to hand
> their ballots through a window and some judges at the voting
> places, after receiving the ballots and before depositing
> them in the ballot-box, performed some little feats of
> legerdemain.[26]

Continuing, the election judge declared that

> at some precincts the ballots had to be handed through
> windows so high from the ground that it was necessary for
> the voter to mount a box or climb a plank to enable him to
> get his head above the window-sill to see the ballot-box.[27]

Interestingly enough, this official found that the practice of election officials in illegally remarking ballots was facetiously styled "mixing the chemicals."[28]

As the Democrats were in charge of the election machinery, they were able to dispose of ballots practically as they pleased.[29] They generally arranged to obtain as watchers for the other party men who were unscrupulous and amenable to their desires. Not infrequently votes were thrown out because of technicalities, such as the misspelling of the candidate's name, or the use of incorrect initials, or because the ticket was marked with the names of the candidate for president and vice-president instead of the presidential electors. As a matter of fact, the votes of entire "precincts might be rejected because the ballots had not been properly strung on a string and sealed."[30]

In addition to blocking the black vote by the above named and similar methods, efforts were usually made to get as many Negroes as possible to vote with the Democrats. Bribery was a favorite way of doing this. The poorer classes of blacks and whites were quite susceptible to selling their ballots for a little tobacco money.[31] However, the strong ties of attachment of the Negro to his church and his minister could often be used much more advantageously in securing votes by purchase. "The usual method of bringing them... was to buy their preachers or other leaders,"[32] who would deliver the solid vote of their followers[33] for a lump sum. This was found to be a much more economical procedure than buying votes individually "for a dollar or for two dollars by the Democrats."[34]

Intimidation Rapidly Intensified

The movement to secure the political impotence of the Negro in Virginia received tremendous impetus as a result of the long and fiery campaign

of John M. Langston in 1888. Race feeling waxed strong as this Negro did
the unprecedented thing of seeking to become one of the Old Dominion's Representatives in the United States Congress.[35] Langston felt that the large
black majority in the Fourth District[36] entitled them to a black Congressman.[37] The Republican State machine, headed by Mahone and beginning to reflect the race prejudice which the reactionaries were tirelessly stirring
up, opposed Langston's nomination. General Mahone was of the opinion,
Langston says, that "no colored man would be allowed to represent the Fourth
Congressional District of Virginia in the Congress of the United States."[38]
Accordingly, the Republican machine was oiled and put into shape because
"the 'nigger' must be beaten at all events..."[39]

John Langston waged an aggressive campaign and was forced to call
on his every resource as he had to buck both the strong Democratic forces
as well as the local Republican leaders who had the support and financial
backing of the national organization. "Every conceivable influence... was
exerted" to defeat the colored candidate.[40] Republican officials brought
pressure to bear and were able to get Fred Douglass and other prominent
Negroes in the party to condemn Langston's action in "bolting" the local
organization.[41] Speaking of the local Republicans who had joined with
Douglass in criticizing Langston, a writer informed the Richmond Dispatch
that Langston's Republican opponents had denounced him in letters to colored
voters. It was stated that these letters "declared that Langston is neither
a negro nor the fit leader of negroes."[42] Continuing, the letters said that
"whilst an official at the national capital Langston declined all association
or affiliation with negroes." The writer concluded that the "Anti-Langston
Republicans were making every possible effort to defeat Langston, and they
will doubtless succeed."[43]

The election was so hotly contested and the Democrats were so
determined to elect their candidate that Langston found it necessary to employ
"quite five hundred persons" to look after his interests on election day.[44]
These helpers, most of whom were paid out of his personal funds, were stat-
ioned in strategic positions at every voting place. They collected sufficient data regarding the manipulation and falsification of ballots to give
factual substantiation to Langston's claims during the crisis that grew out
of the election.

As election day approached, the Democrats again subordinated vital
economic considerations to the "issue" of race. The Dispatch, ever the
mouthpiece of reaction and racial intolerance, lost all of its self-styled
"aversion" to appealing to the racial identity of the readers and hastened to
"remind the voters of Virginia that they are once more called upon to vote
so as to preserve the civilization of the South."[45] Lashing out at both
Langston and his Republican opponents who had candidates in the field, the
editor of the Dispatch, on election eve, completely forgot the history of
Virginia and demanded:

> Will she /Virginia/ Bow cringingly to the yoke of negro
> domination? Has she forgotten the terrible night of recon-
> struction with its hideous saturnalia of robbery, official
> vampirism, and debauchery, its rioting in prejudice,
> passion and hate, its cruel oppression that brought her
> almost to the verge of despair.[46]

All this was said about a State which never had a Negro-Republican Government, which never had a black majority either in the legislature or on the
registration books, which never suffered from a harsh military occupation,
and which witnessed a "restoration" of the State in the very first election
under the Reconstruction Acts. No one would have recognized Virginia as
being the subject of this tirade unless he was completely oblivious to the

course of events in the Old Dominion during the period 1865-1888.

Although backed by an overwhelming majority among the Negroes of the Fourth District, an unfavorable vote was returned for Langston. Venable, the Democratic candidate, was given the election by the Democratic election officials. However, Langston, with a mass of data showing the fraudulent action of the local election officials, was able to successfully contest the decision before the United States House of Representatives.[47] In this election there were several instances in which the polls were closed in the face of long lines of Negroes waiting to cast ballots for Langston.[48]

The election of John Langston to Congress served as good material for the reactionaries in their campaign to eliminate the black voter. The picture of a Negro representing Virginia in the National Legislature was played up to its full emotional and propagandistic value by local demagogues.[49] Here was concrete evidence that "negro domination" was no idle threat. And thus, "it was at this time that the people of Virginia resolved to eliminate them from politics regardless of any means.... They were tired of the danger of friction which their presence in governmental affairs caused."[50]

As the Negroes struggled to prevent their being pushed into political oblivion, the whites, equally determined to effect such, resorted to coercion and terrorism. The charge of rape, "the most unspeakably hideous of all crimes to a Southerner, especially when the offender is of another race,"[51] gave excellent results in stirring up the whites against the Negroes. After 1888 there was a significant increase in lynchings throughout the State. During the period from 1880 to 1888 there were 8 white and 18 colored people lynched in Virginia, 9 of whom were accused of rape and 12 of murder.[52] During the next five years, 1888-1893 the number of lynchings rose to 35, all but five of whom were Negroes.[53] Statistics showing the rapid increase in lynchings in Virginia have been cited as proof of the increased recalcitrance and depravity of the colored people in perpetrating the "unspeakable crime,"[54] and thus the necessity of taking drastic steps against the "black menace." The statistics are offered as definitive evidence of the increase in the crimes at which the lynchings were aimed.[55] The fact was, of course, that it was found that a lynching or two, on the eve of election, was an excellent way of keeping many Negroes from the polls. The Richmond Dispatch, ever paying lip service to the "danger" of "Congo supremacy" and "negro rule, " justified and white washed the outbursts of mob terrorism at every opportunity. On one occasion the editor bragged that recently "we printed an article showing that lynch law is the only law that can with the consent of the community be relied upon in those cases in which negroes commit the unspeakable crime upon women."[56] After several paragraphs of diatribe the Dispatch concludes: "We reserve lynch law for the unspeakable crime."[57]

Lynching became an effective instrument of intimidation and was thus an important weapon in the hands of the reactionaries. Cognizant of this, the Governor of Virginia, in a message to the Legislature, December 6, 1893, stated that the whites were solidly in control with the government firmly held in their hand, and that thus there was no longer any excuse for mob rule. This admonishment from the high office of the Governor is proof in itself that the hideous act of lynching was being frequently utilized to terrorize the Negro into respecting "white supremacy" and keeping out of politics. And, inhuman as this practice was, white "men's consciences became more or less accustomed to such methods."

CHAPTER VIII

POPULISM AND THE MOVEMENT TOWARD LEGISLATIVE ELIMINATION

Under ordinary conditions the whites found little diffuculty in maintaining their control over the government of the State. It was during the period of the revolt within white ranks that the Negro became such an important and feared political force. These periods, however, were few and far between as the reactionaries constantly kept before the whites the duty and necessity of supporting the "white man's party" in order that Virginia remain "a white man's State." But effective as this appeal was there were occasional conflicts in which the Democrats, in response to conflicting interests, would divide along class lines. And after a decade of loyalty to the "Solid South," Virginia faced the possibility of white solidarity being shattered by the agrarian movement which was sweeping the West and Middle West in the late 80's and early 90's.[1]

Virginia, like most of the other agricultural States, was undergoing an intense period of agrarian depression in the years after the Civil War. And the almost complete preoccupation of the national government with matters favorable to the expansion and growth of the "new industrialism"[2] was drawing the criticism of the small farmers of Virginia as well as other agrarian sections. The Old Dominion was also suffering from an outworn system of land tenure. Particularly was this true of the Southside where the Black Belt cut a dark path through the terrain of the State. In this section share-cropping had gained a firm hold after the Civil War.[3] In 1890 it was reported that in Pittsylvania, a county of the Black Belt, fifty per cent of the farmers were share-croppers,[4] half being white and half colored.

This undiversified system of agriculture contributed to the extremely distressing condition which existed in Virginia during this period.

The first outburst of agrarian "radicalism" occurred in the latter part of the 1880's when the Farmers' Alliances gained a foothold in the State. It has been variously estimated that the membership of this organization totaled from 35,000 to 80,000.[5] It is said that there were between 5,000 and 20,000 Negroes in the State branches of the Colored Farmers' Alliance, the parallel national organization.[6] These organizations of farmers, however, did not become really significant as a political force in the State until 1890, at which time they lost their secret and non-partisan nature and went openly into politics.

The agitation in the Southside, the seat of agrarian unrest in the State, did not become really articulare until 1892, at which time Populism began a fight for farm relief. But even though there was widespread distress and signs of political revolt, the Populists were unable to break through the artificial barriers of race and social practice. The Democrats, genuinely afraid of this popular movement which had come out of the West, immediately realized that "Bourbon" control was threatened. And, as of yore, they conjured up the danger of the Negro's "return to power."[7] The whites were exhorted to maintain their solidarity at all costs. They were told that should they divide "Mahone and the negro"[8] would again "control" the political destiny of the State. Among the outbursts of violence which accompanied the reactionary propaganda about the new threat of "negro domination" was an incident at Roanoke in which a riot resulted from the attempts of the militia to prevent the lynching of a Negro. Eight people were killed in the ensuing disturbance.[9]

Fundamental economic problems were completely subordinated to the "race question."[10] "The man blessed with a white cuticle is false if he does not in this emergency cooperate with the Democratic party,"[11] was the challenge of one speaker. The election returns of 1892 and 1893 resulted in Democratic victories. Although the Populists elected several[12] men to the legislature in the latter year, they were unable to achieve the success of the agrarians in other southern and western states.[13] Partly responsible for Populist lack of success was the fraudulent manner in which many of their votes were handled. In keeping with the usual practice of eliminating opposition, "many Populist ballots were destroyed because of minor technicalities."[14] The chief Populist support came from the Southside, which included the Black Belt. The Democrats, therefore, were in a very favorable position because they had had long experience in nullifying the Negro vote in this section. In the "partisan manipulations of elections which followed" the "returns of precincts in which Goode /the Populist candidate7 led had been omitted on the basis of such trivialities as failure to tie correctly the bundle in which ballots were sent to the state supervisors."[15] And, we are informed, "Its sole excuse was that supposedly only by such trickery and deceit could white supremacy be assured..."[16]

Once again the reactionaries had broken a revolt in the ranks of the Democracy by means of raising the black scare. Again the aspirations of a depressed class had been frustrated in traditional manner. Thus, many whites, oblivious of a realistic solution to their economic problems, laid their troubles at the door of the Negro. It was inevitable, therefore, that the reaction should give new impetus to the movement to get the black voter totally out of the arena of politics. The Populist had decried the waving of the "bloody shirt,"[17] and had vainly attempted to prove that the "great issues of today have nothing to do with the struggle of 1861-1865."[18] But the tide of emotional appeals, traditional hatreds and accepted modes of action were overwhelming. Thus it was not unexpected that many Populists, broken and disillusioned, came to advocate that it was best that the Negro be excluded from politics. The vital difference between the Populists and the reactionaries was that for the latter disfranchisement of the Negro would mean their continued domination, while for the former it would mean a possible chance to solve basic economic problems by means of a politico-economic program.

The Walton Act

Violence and fraud had been so extensively used in "safe-guarding" the State against the "black threat" especially in the "negro counties"[19] that a further extension of this type of activity offered little hope of success. The political corruption and fraudulent elections which regularly occurred in Virginia were drawing criticism from both outside and inside the State.[20] Democratic leaders, therefore, decided that much of the results they were achieving by intimidation and fraud could be in great part accomplished by the less strenuous method of elimination by legislative enactment. Accordingly, sentiment for an election law that would disfranchise a larger part of the black electorate gained steadily. This movement was encouraged by the growing demand for relief from the Anderson-McCormick Act. Although it was "a fact... that this law was understood by the people to be passed in order that negroes in the lower counties might be cheated out of their votes,"[21] its administration had affected many white votes. It had been used to frustrate any opposition within white ranks, especially in those sections where the whites embraced Republicanism. This weapon of legal disfranchisement had been extensively used to subdue the agrarian revolt[22] ushered in by Populism, at which time many Populist votes were nullified.[23] Cognizant of the corruption around him, one editor declared emphatically that "... cheating in elections is demoralizing our whole people...."[24]

Taking advantage of the widespread demands for election reforms the Democratic Legislature drew up the Walton bill. This measure, proposing to "secure decent and honest elections...", was primarily designed "to eliminate the most objectionable of the voters...."[25] The Dispatch convinced that "Virginia will rue the day when they submit to the delusion that the negro is no longer to be feared in Virginia politics",[26] was delighted at the proposed bill and stated, encouragingly, that "... if in the judgment of the /white/ people of the 'negro belt' it will work well, we feel certain that the people of other sections of the state will aid them to pass it."[27]

To help secure a favorable decision on the proposed election bill, a prominent Winchester politician announced that the provisions of the Walton Act were quite similar to the election laws which had been in effect in his section "for several years."[28] "As soon as the Australian system went into effect," he stated, "there was an immediate change.... The result was that the negroes in Winchester have practically ceased voting in municipal elections, and the town invariably goes Democratic."[29] The writer was thus able to conclude: "From our experience in Winchester, I believe that the Walton Bill is decidedly favorable to good government and white supremacy."[30]

The Walton Act, passed March 2, 1894,[31] introduced a modified version of the Australian ballot. It provided that official printed ballots be prepared by an election board and delivered to the polls sealed. Private

booths were to be provided so that electors could mark their votes in
secrecy. No one but the voter and election officials were allowed within 40
feet of the booths. Each voter was given two and a half minutes in which to
prepare his ballot. And in the event the elector was educationally or
physically unable to mark his ballot, he could obtain the assistance of a
"special constable" who was provided for that purpose. The law stipulated
that in order to mark the ballot correctly, a line had to be drawn at least
three-fourths of the way through the names of the candidates for whom the
elector was not voting. The bill specified that the ballots were to contain
no symbols or other party designations.[32]

The new election law received a favorable vote on March 3, after
facing the vain attempts of some members of the Assembly to amend it so
as to exempt their counties from conforming to the act.[33] The next day
the Dispatch, observing that "negro rule is a terrible thing," stated that
while the Walton Act had superceded the tried and true "white man's law"
embodied in the Anderson-McCormick Act, it was to be hoped that the new
legislation "will offer relief to a long-suffering and much-misrepresented
white people...." of the "negro belt."[34]

The Walton Act offered an improved mechanical set-up for the State's
election machinery in that official ballots were provided for and secrecy in
voting made possible. Again, the law made bribery and the purchase of votes
more difficult. If a candidate could not observe how an elector voted he
would, in all probability, hesitate about making advance payment for the
vote. Nominally, fraudulent balloting was curtailed, but nothing prevented
the election officials from "fixing" the returns, as they had done so
successfully in past years.[35]

In terms of its purpose--of which McDaniel says that "few attempts were made to deny that it was designed to disfranchise the illiterate colored voters,"[36] -- the law proved very effective. The provision for "special constables" to aid those who were educationally or physically incapacitated was a legal farce; it killed two birds with one stone: First, it was inserted to insure the constitutionality of the legislation, and, second, to put the illiterate voter at the mercy of the election official, who would mark the ballot as he chose. With 57.2 per cent of Negroes of Virginia being illiterate, it is obvious that the Negro vote must inevitably suffer under the new law. As predicted by the Winchester politician, the new election law gave immediate and definite results. In the words of the Governor of the State:

> Many illiterate voters were practically disfranchised by the Walton law in spite of the fact that they could receive official assistance if necessary. Negroes often hesitated in getting a Democratic election judge to assist them in marking their ballots; others were timid or ashamed to acknowledge their ignorance; and many who attempted to vote could not correctly mark their ballots in the alloted time. In some precincts from a third to half of the ballots had to be thrown out because they were incorrectly prepared.[37]

It is both interesting and significant to note that the Republican vote for governor of the State, after having been 120,477 in 1889, dropped to 56,840 in 1897.[38]

The Walton Act further opened "the door for wholesale corruption." Contrary to what had been claimed, "Under the operation of this law many of the same practices which had been used before were used to cut down the negro vote."[39] Lines of colored voters were still delayed by incessant challenges and in heavily black districts there was still an acute shortage of ballot-boxes. The "special constables" who exercised almost plenary power in executing the election law, often refused

> to mark the ballots (of Negroes) on the grounds that the law
> only gave them authority to mark ballots for those physically
> unable to do so. For others they would read the ballots,
> pointing out the positions of the names on the ballots as
> they read them.[40]

The provisions of the law enabled the election officials to take advantage of a myriad of technicalities. For example, many ballots were thrown out because the lines were not marked three-fourths of the way through the names and because they were not drawn through three-fourths of the letters of the name, and sometimes even "because the line was not straight."[41] In an election in the Tenth District later in the year of 1894, the official ballots in two counties were printed in German and script type.[42] After much protest from both white and black voters the Walton Act was amended in 1896 to require that the names of the candidates should be printed in the same, regular order and in plain Roman type.[43]

The constitutionality of the Walton Act was immediately contested. In this case[44] it was charged that the act was invalid because "it establishes physical and educational qualifications for electors in violation of Article 3, section 1, of the Constitution of Virginia... because the act deprives the electors of equality of civil and political rights and public privileges..."[45] and because the two and a half minutes allowed was insufficient time in which to mark the complicated ballot. Upon appeal from the decision of the Circuit Court in favor of the defendants, the Supreme Court of Appeals of Virginia, sustaining the decision of the lower tribunal, upheld the validity of the new election law. Recognizing the fact that the "special constables" were given great initiative and power, and that such power "is liable to be abused," the Court did "not think, however, that all the

elaborate provisions of the act in question are but artful expedients con-
trived for the purpose of deluding, entrapping, and defrauding the ignorant
voters of this commonwealth."[46]

The justices found that the two and a half minute time limit was
adequate for preparing a ballot[47] and decided that

> Whether or not the rules and regulations, the checks and safe-
> guards with which the legislature has seen fit to surround the
> exercise of the right of suffrage in order to secure a full,
> free, and untrammeled expression of the will of the voter are
> the best that could be devised, is not for us to decide. Such
> arguments must be addressed to the law-making power.[48]

The "white man's law" , devised to guarantee "white supremacy," thus received
judicial approbation.

CHAPTER IX

THE MOVEMENT TOWARD DISFRANCHISEMENT BY REVISION OF THE ORGANIC LAW

By 1900 the Negro had been eliminated as a factor of primary importance in the politics of the Old Dominion. Even in the Black Belt--the last stronghold of effective black political influence, he had seen his power diminished to the vanishing point. One writer was able to report that in the 1896 elections "the Democrats _had_ _their_ _own_ _way_ in all the black counties...."[1] Notwithstanding the fact that the Negro voter had been reduced to a state of political impotence, the Democrats were still unsatisfied. Flushed with repeated success in their efforts to disfranchise him, they desired to push the movement to an effective culmination. Having the Negro down, they wished to make it impossible for him to ever rise again. The Democrats also wanted to guard against any split within their ranks which might, with the aid of the colored people, challenge the domination of the Democracy. Memories of the successful revolt of "Readjusterism" and the threatened agrarian rebellion of 1892-95 were disturbing to the old line politicians.

There were also those who, though desirous of seeing the Negro totally removed from politics, believed that it should be accomplished by other than fraud and coercion. Drawing a somewhat dubious and farfetched moral distinction between corrupt and fraudulent practices of "counting out" black votes and the elimination of the black voter by statute, this group advocated "legally" getting around the law. They viewed with alarm the ever-growing corruption and maladministration in Virginia and felt, mistakenly that the wholesome development of democratic institutions would be stimulated by working "within" the law in the disfranchisement of the Negro. Morton

writes:

> In spite of the fact that the white people of Virginia had
> practically taken the vote from the Negroes by the middle
> of the 90's, they were greatly dissatisfied with political
> conditions as they existed. The system of fraud that had
> been built up to defeat Mahoneism by disfranchising the
> negroes had a demoralizing effect upon the whole electoral
> system, and was finally used where whites alone were concerned.[2]

Virginia's sorry record between 1870 and 1900 led many to ask for

a political "housecleaning." During this period there were 20 contested

elections[3] in the lower house of Congress. Of these "four dealt with the

eligibility of the contestants on the interpretation of the Virginia

election law of 1894; the 16 dealt with alleged fraud."[4] In some of these

cases, contested before a Republican House, several Democrats lost or were

not allowed to retain their seats. Of one such instance, the Richmond Times,

long an exponent of "legal" disfranchisement, stated:

> The same arguments of fraud in elections is sufficient in
> every case before a partisan House to evict a Democrat and
> seat a Republican.... The only remedy is in the qualification
> of suffrage so as to eliminate the negro vote, and then the
> only justification--if that be sufficient--for fraudulent
> elections will be removed.[5]

Finding encouragement in many quarters, sentiment for calling a

constitutional convention to bring the State's organic law into closer

affinity with the tenets of "white supremacy," gained considerably. How-

ever, such sentiment had by no means become overwhelming. Agitation for

holding a constitutional convention had begun shortly after the return of

the reactionaries to power in 1870. Although resolutions to amend the

Constitution or to take the vote of the people on calling a constitutional

convention had been offered at every session since 1874, enough support in the legislature to submit the issue could not be obtained until 1888. The organic law of 1867-1868 provided that no convention for the purpose of altering the constitution should take place before 1888.[6] Upon submission to the people in 1888, the proposal was defeated by a vote of 63,125 to 3,698.[7]

The convention issue was also submitted to the electorate in 1897 and was again defeated, this time by a vote of 83,435 to 38,326.[8] As before, there was little interest in the campaign. By 1900, however, the forces of reaction were speeding up their efforts to create sentiment for a convention. On the 6th of May of that year, in the Richmond Times we see the following: "If the Democratic Party continues its revolutionary election tactics the party will be irreparably split," and further that "if a split is to come it had far better come with the negro vote out of the way than with the black menace hanging over us."[9]

Sentiment for calling a convention developed sufficient strength in the Democratic caucas of 1900 to make possible the successful passage of a bill, approved May 5, 1900, to submit the issue to the approval of the people once more.[10] Its proponents were determined that the issue should not receive the cold reception which it had drawn on former occasions. A clever ruse was hit upon to help secure its approval. "In order to give the measure all the assistance possible,"[11] the legislature provided that the ballots should only bear the words: "For Constitutional Convention."[12] In order to vote against holding the convention, it was necessary to mark out these words. Any ballot that was unmarked was counted as a vote in favor of the convention. A further important tactical step made by the leaders of the Democracy was the attempt to obtain the endorsement of the State Democratic Convention for the measure. This would make the calling of a convention

primarily a party issue and, with the Republicans constituting the chief
opposition, it would mean a Democratic victory and thus a favorable vote.
After considerable debate, the Democratic Convention, meeting at Norfolk,
adopted the following resolution:

> Whereas the General Assembly of Virginia has submitted to the
> vote of the people the question of the calling of a constitu-
> tional convention, and whereas, it is the evident desire of
> the people of Virginia to amend and revise the present
> constitution;
>
> Resolved, That the Democratic Party, in convention
> assembled, endorse the action of the General Assembly, and
> urgently urge the people of Virginia to vote on the fourth
> Thursday for calling a constitutional convention.[13]

To help secure the approval of the poorer whites, especially in the Blue
Ridge sections, it was also

> Resolved, That is is the sense of this convention that
> in framing a new constitution no effort should be made to
> disfranchise any citizen of Virginia who had a right to
> vote prior to 1861, nor the descendent of any such person,
> and that when such a constitution shall have been framed,
> it shall be submitted to a vote of the people for ratifica-
> tion or rejection....[14]

Opponents of the Convention

There were three main sources of opposition to the convention.
First in number and importance, were the black electors, who knew that the
object of calling the convention was to further prescribe them in the
exercise of their constitutional rights. Secondly, there were the poor whites
of the western hills--a stronghold of both illiteracy and Republicanism.
Having a greater amount of illiteracy than among the Negroes, they feared
that any constitutional change which would exclude the colored voter could
and would be used against them. And the past--especially the capitation
tax of 1876, the Anderson-McCormick bill, the Walton law, etc.--indicated
that these fears were well founded. Indeed, most of the white criticism of

these measures resulted from the fact that they had worked to eliminate thousands of the whites.[15] The white Republicans were naturally opposed to a convention inasmuch as any constitutional revision would reduce their already small vote. They exhorted the voters to defeat the projected "outrage." Fourthly, there was a group of Democrats who, for various reasons, opposed a convention. Among these there were many who realized the "scare-all" value of the Negro vote as a means of insuring "white supremacy" by maintaining while solidarity, and thus perpetuating Democratic domination. This element, then as now, utilized racial antagonism as an instrument for safeguarding one-party control of the South. Concisely stating this point of view, the Richmond Times said that many Democrats believed

> and with considerable foundation for their belief, that the elimination of the negro as a voting factor means the dis-integration of the Democrats who have been held together by antipathy to the black race. They think the Republican party without the negro will gain large accessions from the respectable white element in the State, and thus Democratic supremacy will be threatened.[16]

Also among this group were some Democratic county and city office-holders who, out of self-interest, objected to the proposed plan to abolish many of the county and city offices. A local paper stated that "office holders.... are trying to defeat the constitutional revision by the policy of silence."[17] However, most of the opposition from this quarter was stifled when the Democratic Convention went on record in favor of the revision of the constitution. Finally, there were those who, seeing the real condition of the black electorate, felt that a convention for the purpose of further excluding the Negro was totally unnecessary.

Convention Victorious

The convention issue was to be decided on May 24, at which time the people were to make their decision. After a spirited battle the convention was returned victor by a vote of 77,362 to 60,375.[18] It was at once apparent that the announced election figures had been achieved by means of manipulation and intimidation. An indication of the flagrant fraud that occurred is shown by the itemized account of the vote distribution. Returns of the vote, completely contrary to what could have been expected, showed that 19 counties with preponderantly black population--ranging from 50.8 per cent to 70 per cent Negroes--had voted, in most cases by large majorities, in favor of the convention. For example, Charlotte County, with a population of 6,798 whites and 8,545 Negroes--55.6 per cent, voted for the convention by 612 to 132.[19]

Again, the convention had been successful in spite of the fact that many overwhelmingly white counties voted almost solidly against it.[20] Seventeen such counties, having only from .005 per cent to 10.8 per cent Negroes flatly repudiated the convention.[21] Typical of this group was Shennandoah County, which contained 19,604 whites and 649 (3.20 per cent) Negroes. There the vote was 1,093 against the convention to 569 in favor.[22] Therefore, faced with defeat in many of the white counties, the proponents of the convention found it necessary to secure a favorable vote in the Black Belt. And no trickery, it appears, was omitted in excluding Negro voters and manipulating the ballots of those who were able to vote. It is impossible to explain in any other manner the situation in which many Negroes, knowing that a constitutional convention would mean another attack on the rights for which they had long struggled, had either voted for the convention or refrained from voting altogether. Realizing the illogicality of such action, the Richmond Times was disposed to admit that in many counties the colored ballots were not counted and that the Negro was generally "encouraged not to vote."[23]

The election of delegates to the proposed convention was set for May 23, 1910,[24] and in the interim the Democrats worked out comprehensive plans for this final, "knockout" assault on the black electorate. Advice and suggestions came from many quarters.[25] Perhaps the most interesting of the suggestions for the forthcoming convention were made by one A. F. Thomas, of Lynchburg, who wrote a most interesting pamphlet entitled, "The Virginia Constitutional Convention and Its Possibilities." In this monograph Thomas, later to become a State Senator, outlined a comprehensive program for the convention. Referring to the 15th Amendment, he observed that

> Thirty years after its adoption, the negro race has less
> political rights than it had then.... Today the negro
> has no political rights which the white man feels called
> upon to respect, if that right involves in the slightest
> degree the possibility of negro domination or even
> political equality.[26]

Conceiving of the solution to the "negro problem" to lie in segregation, subordination, or extermination," Thomas contended that education is useless because it elevates the negro, hence renders him less tractable and less willing to fulfil the duties of a subservient class, hence it widens the chasm between the races...."[27] In keeping with Virginia's fast developing policy of rigid racial parallelism, the author believed that the way out of the situation would be to "conceive of a plan for segregation by which the negro might have autonomy and be left to fulfil his destiny...."[28] (which was to serve the white man). "Realizing the necessity of eliminating the negro from politics" and even "of divesting him of his nominal citizenship," Thomas states that "we should do something to accomplish these ends."[29] In the final analysis, this would make very little difference any way, he said, as "The loss of the right to vote would not affect the negro, because votes are not effective unless counted."[30] With characteristic frankness

Thomas states that

> It is an open secret that the negro's vote is rendered
> nugatory wherever it is sufficiently large to endanger
> white supremacy. If he votes enough to be effective, the
> white race circumvents him by the easiest method--fraud,
> if possible, force, if necessary.[31]

Although Thomas was convinced that "our government" should "extend
its citizenship to the white race only,"[32] he did not care to see the Negro
disfranchised by legislation. While the 15th Amendment stood as "a monument
to the ignorance, folly and perhaps maliciousness of its authors," he believed that "To disregard and violate it in our State constitution would
place the state in the attitude of lawbreaker... no condition would justify
this," because "Respect for the law is the foundation stone of government."[33]
He therefore advocated that the exclusion of the Negro be accomplished by
"individual"[34] effort until the repeal of the 15th Amendment could be
achieved. Thomas was firmly convinced that "No provision of a State Constitution that would destroy this guarantee the right of the Negro to vote would
stand any chance before an intelligent and honest court."[35] However, in the
light of subsequent opinions of the Supreme Court, one is inclined to wonder
as to just which of Thomas' adjectives these learned gentlemen failed to
measure up.

Anticipating the culmination of the long fight to frustrate the
black elector, the Richmond Times, after demanding the repeal of the 15th
Amendment, editorailized:

> The people of the South, have determined that the Negro shall
> not continue to be a disturbing factor in their politics, and
> they are going to disfranchise him whether or not the 15th
> Amendment be repealed.... Virginia is taking steps to
> accomplish that end. The Fifteenth Amendment will soon be a
> dead letter so far as the Southern States are concerned.[36]

CHAPTER X

THE DISFRANCHISING CONSTITUTIONAL CONVENTION OF 1901-1902

The struggle to remove every semblance of political prestige and power from the Negro by revision of the state Constitution was under way. The papers daily carried half page articles by prominent local politicians showing in detail the progress of the movement for black disfranchisement in the South.[1] On the 12th of June, 1901, the 100 delegates assembled in convention;[2] of these, 88 were Democrats and 12 were Republicans.[3] This distinguished assemblage contained no Negroes. There was not the slightest hesitation in manifesting the task which had been undertaken. The single-ness of purpose to which the convention was dedicated was expressed by one delegate when he said, ".... we are making an effort to find, within the limits of the law, a method of escaping from a constitutional policy exactly contrary to the purpose and the wishes of the Virginia people."[4] And although an arduous session was forecast in which sectional rivalry would cause great difficulty, there was an unanimity of opinion that

> No matter what the costs, no matter what the method, this
> one fact stands out supremely true, that the Anglo-Saxon
> race is now and will be forever master wherever it exists.[5]

As the convention was about to get down to business, an interest-ing controversy developed out of the attitude of some of the delegates toward the oath required by the constitution of 1867-68. This instrument specified that

> All persons before entering upon the discharge of any functions
> as officers of this State, must take and subscribe to the
> following oath or affirmation:
>
> I, _____ _____, do solemnly swear (or affirm)

> that I will support and maintain the Constitution and
> laws of the United States and Constitution and laws
> of the State of Virginia; that I recognize and accept
> the civil and political equality of all men before the
> law, and that I will faithfully perform the duty of
> _____ to the best of my ability. So help me
> God.[6]

Obviously, this oath could not be taken, or, if taken, could not

be adhered to, and the purposes of the convention be carried out. A few

of the delegates questioned the propriety as well as the legality of

taking an oath to a constitution to which they were pledged to emasculate.[7]

Others felt that the holiness of their purpose stood prior to any mere

ethical or legal consideration such as this. As a whole, the delegates

were in no mood to be frustrated or even long impeded by catering to

points of law. They were there to break the law and not to conform to it.

After some half-hearted, though at times fervent, debate into which the

Republicans entered spiritedly, the motion requiring that the members take

the oath was tabled.[8]

To aid the convention in executing its work, a clever little hand-

book, entitled "The Virginia Constitutional Convention Directory, 1901" was

provided. This "directory contained, among other things, a complete list

of the suffrage clauses which Mississippi, South Carolina, Louisiana, and

North Carolina had recently created as a means of disfranchising their

black population.

It was a difficult situation which confronted the convention in

the pursuit of its chosen task. The Negro was to be eliminated but the

method accomplishing this offered far more difficulty than many anticipated.

The geographic differentiation and sectional antipathy of the State were

decisively complicating factors. Almost all of the Negro population was concentrated in the East and Southeast--the Black Belt area; 35 counties

had black majorities. There were 65 counties having white majorities and

many of these were beyond the Blue Ridge where the poorer whites and

Republicanism held forth. Since the "suffrage situation" was so completely

different in the various sections of the State, finding a single plan which

would be applicable to all of them was, indeed, a problem.

There was objection to using the educational or literary test

alone because of the rapid rate at which illiterary was diminishing among

the Negroes of the State. It was estimated that between 1890 and 1900, the

illiteracy of the colored population was reduced by 25 per cent, having

dropped from a little more than 57 per cent in the former year to a fraction

over 31 per cent in 1900.[9] An excerpt from the report of an educator was

quoted to show that

> The interest of negroes in education is immense. They have
> discovered that it is the ladder on which they must arise.
> Both children and parents are making great sacrifice to
> secure it. The enrollment of colored children in the
> schools has immensely increased. In some districts they
> literally fill the doors and windows of the school house.[10]

Some of the delegates had other objections to the educational

test. They believed that even if such a test were administered so as not

to exclude the illiterate whites--the fear of representatives from the

western sections--it would eliminate the old-time "faithful" Negroes and

favor the young colored men who could read and write-- "the gingercake

school graduate--with a diploma of side whiskers and beaver hat, pocket

pistols, brass knucks, and bicycles....."[11] To make a law which would hit

the "faithful" Negroes and favor the younger ones was deplorable, one

delegate said, because "we may forego to visit the iniquities of the fathers

upon the children, but we cannot punish those who have obeyed us and kept our commandments."[12]

Should it be necessary, however, the delegate was willing to
sacrifice the "old-Timer" in order to get at the young "ginger-cake school
graduate" because

> I believe today, as I have ever believed, that it is to the
> interest of both races in this commonwealth that the
> political rights of the negro should be wholly withdrawn,
> and if I had it in my power, in behalf of the negro himself,
> I would repeal that article in the National Constitution
> which confers suffrage rights upon him, because, Mr.
> President, the negro's ballot does him no good, and only
> increases the points of conflict and of friction between
> him and us in this great struggle which we are waging for
> supremacy and for white dominion everywhere.[13]

Advocates of a poll tax proposed that it be instituted as a method
of proscribing the negro vote. It was generally conceded, however, that
this alone would be ineffective. Again, the

> .... requirement of a poll tax prerequisite will be, at best
> in those western communities a hardship upon the white
> race. There are some portions of the State of Virginia in
> which ready money is handled to a larger extent by the
> negroes than by the white people.[14]

Unable to tell "where it will strike nor what its effects will
be," the situation was further complicated by the problem of Negro organization. As a delegate stated:

> .... the negro race is organized from one end of this State
> to the other in a way that is impossible among the white
> race. They are organized everywhere and controlled every-
> where through the power of their church. You can give
> notice of anything that is to happen tomorrow night in
> almost any county in this Commonwealth, and it will, before
> that time, be known from one end of the county to the other
> by the negroes.... and it will be an easy thing, when the
> negro realizes that there is nothing except the poll tax
> between him and the ballot-box, for the churches to organize
> that race six months in advance, and, we fear, to make the
> negroes pay a poll tax in larger proportion than the white
> people will.[15]

In the course of this discussion a delegate to the convention

made a brilliant statement of Virginia's policy of racial separatism and
the status of the Negro as a victim of segregation and proscription.
Pointing out the inadequacy of a suggested $1.50 poll tax and an educat-
ional test as the only qualifications for the franchise, the enraged delegate, desiring more, said:

> Having for the past ten years been familiar with the
> negro as a voter, and as a practical politician, I cannot, I
> do not believe that offers any adequate protection to my
> people.
> We put ourselves in the attitude of the negro on this
> question, and what conclusion do we come to? We must
> remember that this is his <u>highest</u> personal privilege. When
> he sends his children to school he must send them to a
> separate schoolhouse; when he goes to worship, it is to a
> separate church; when he takes the railroad to travel, he
> must take a separate coach. <u>At all times and in all
> places</u> he <u>is</u> separated--subordinated. It is only at the
> ballot-box that he meets you face to face on terms of
> absolute equality. Is there any man who has spent his
> life among those people, any reasonable Virginian, familiar
> with the characteristics of that race, who is willing to
> stand here and say he believes in his heart that the negro
> will forego that privilege and waive his highest claim of
> freedom and equality for the paltry sum of one dollar and
> fifty cents?[16]

In the end the poll tax was to be accepted as a requisite to the
franchise, but only as a partial requirement; the convention looked around
for additional qualifications. To the objection that a provision requiring
electors to possess at least $200 worth of taxable property would work a
hardship on many voters, the reply was made that "we never could get rid
of the negro vote in this state without some sacrifice, however small, of
the white vote."[17]

The convention developed considerable sentiment in favor of
writing an "understanding clause"[18] into the Constitution to debar the
black electorate. In regard to such a clause, Mr. Thom stated that while
it was not ideal it "is efficient to do this work."[19] Referring to the

proposal that ex-soldiers and owners of property above $200 be exempted from

taking the "understanding" test, it was explained that

> The two classes with which it is an alternative are the
> soldier class and the property-holding class, and through
> neither of these gateways will any large number of negroes
> ever be able to approach the ballot-box. So that if any
> considerable number of negroes come into suffrage it must
> be through this "understanding clause"--a "gateway" which
> could be opened and shut at the whim of the white election
> officials.[20]

To those who doubted the effectiveness of the "understanding

clause," it was explained that "we think that it will be efficient because

we do not believe that the negro can stand this examination."[21] But even if

a considerable number of Negroes should be able to meet the letter of the

law, the situation offered no great problem. It was deliberately planned

that in such an event the administration of the law would, in this event,

act as the powerful impediment to Negro suffrage. Admitting this, Delegate

Thom said

> .... it would not be frank in me, Mr. Chairman, if I did
> not say that I do not expect an understanding clause to be
> administered with any degree of friendship by the white man to
> the suffrage of the black man. I expect the examination
> with which the black man will be confronted, to be inspired by
> the same spirit that inspires every man upon this floor and
> in this convention. I would not expect an impartial administra-
> tion of the clause.[22]

Continuing the remarkable frankness and disregard for any

semblance of justice which characterized the Convention, Thom further stated

that

> I would not expect for the white man a rigid examination. The
> people of Virginia do not stand impartially between the suffrage
> of the white man and the suffrage of the black man. If they
> did, this Convention would not be assembled upon this floor. If
> they did, the uppermost thoughts in the hearts of every man with-
> in the sound of my voice would not be to find a way of disfran-
> chising the black man and enfranchising the white man. We do
> not come here promoted by an impartial purpose in reference to

negro suffrage. We come here to sweep the field of expedients for the purpose of finding some constitutional method of ridding ourselves of it forever; and we have the approval of the Supreme Court of the United States in making that effort.[23]

Another point in favor of an "understanding clause" was the psychological effect it would have on the black voter, a condition which, it was believed, would greatly add to its thoroughness. Delegate Thom made it plain that

.... I expect this clause to be efficient, because it will act 'in terrorem' upon the negro race. They believe that they will have a hostile examination put upon them by the white man, and they believe that that will be a preventive to their exercising the right of suffrage, and they will not apply for registration.[24]

It was agreed that a few Negroes, as individuals, might be able to meet the proposed requirements and force their way into the franchise. Such was quite possible, theoretically, because, as one delegate said, in the event that a colored elector "is improperly excluded in any individual instance, then the machinery established here, by this very Constitution is sufficient for his protection."[25] Reference was here being made to the provision for a method of appeal from the decisions of the registrars. This, however, was merely a concession to, or rather a blind for, constitutionality. As a few individuals the black voters were not feared. It was as a steadily progressing group that they met opposition. Speaking of the general movement toward disfranchisement of the Negro by constitutional revision, the editor of the Atlantic Monthly said of this tendency that many of the poor whites, ignorant and "who are being outstripped in the march of civilization even by the Negroes," probably do, "imagine that a 'grand-father clause' will save them from the consequences of illiteracy and degeneracy."[26]

A section in the new Constitution provided that if a person with the

necessary qualifications should be excluded from registration, he might "appeal
to the Judge of the Circuit Court, who, if he is wronged by the registration
officer, can at once correct the wrong the for negro as well as for the white
man."[27] Knowing that few Negroes would be able or inclined to make the
sacrifices necessary to penetrate these barriers, the convention was assured
that the black masses neither could nor would form a threat since "all this
will be an effective impediment in the way of the negro, because his tenacity
of purpose will not be sufficient to bring him into the suffrage as a race."[28]

In reality, of course, the provision for an appeal to the courts
was inserted for two reasons: first, it was designed to help bolster the
chance of a favorable reception by the Supreme Court; second, it was intended
to act as a reassurance to the poorer whites. A delegate pointed out that

> This clause will not exclude any worthy white citizen of
> this Commonwealth from the suffrage; for the white man
> is friendly to the white man's suffrage; and the white
> man will find a friendly examiner when he goes to stand
> this examination. We believe, in addition to that, that
> if it is not so, that here stands the Circuit Judge, with
> his chambers always open, to give the white man the right
> which might have been improperly denied him by the
> registration officer.[29]

The basic opposition to the "understanding clause" came from the
representatives of the poorer whites and it was to this element that
apologies were again directed. Seeking their acquiescence, they were told
that, far from being aimed at their constituents, this clause was "intended
to open to the illiterate white men of Virginia an avenue to the ballot-box."[30]
And it was no easy task to convince these men that their people "beyond the
mountains" would not also be the victims of this effort to rid the polls of
the black voter. Ending a long and earnest debate, delegate Thom concluded
by reiterating that the proposed plan

is intended to let into the suffrage the illiterate white
men whom these gentlemen of the minority more especially
represent.... We say we are hand in hand with you on the
purpose of bringing your white men to the polls, but, at
the same time, we say, forget not gentlemen, the problem
that is upon us, and concede the same thing to us, for
the purpose of excluding our black men from the polls.[31]

As the historic convention neared its end, Carter Glass, the man
who had been the dominant and guiding spirit behind the movement to completely
eliminate the Negro by constitutional provision, arose triumphant to assure
and predict that "in the midst of differing contentions and suggested
perplexities, there stands out the uncontroverted fact that the article of
suffrage which the Convention will today adopt does not necessarily deprive
a single white man of the ballot, but will inevitably out from the existing
electorate four-fifths of the negro voters. That was the purpose of the
Convention; that will be its achievement."[32]

When a fellow delegate, out of naivete or temerity, inquired as to
whether this exclusion of the colored electorate was not being "done by fraud
and discrimination?", Mr. Glass retorted: "By fraud, no; by discrimination,
yes. But it will be discrimination within the letter of the law, and not in
the violation of the law. Discrimination! Why, that is precisely what we
propose; that, exactly, is what this Convention was elected for--to discriminate
to the very extremity of permissible action under the limitations of the
Federal Constitution, with a view to the elimination of every negro voter who
can be gotten rid of, legally, without materially impairing the numerical
strength of the white electorate."[33]

In conclusion, however, Delegate Glass added as a sort of farcical
after-thought:

As has been said, we have accomplished our purpose strictly
within the limitations of the Federal Constitution by

legislating against characteristics of the black race, and not
against the "race, color or previous condition" of the people
themselves. It is a fine discrimination, indeed, that we have
practiced in the fabrication of this plan....[34]

The spokesman for delegates from the Negro districts and those from the

Republican West, realizing that they had lost their fight, expressed a last,

hopeless dissent:

.... I was of the opinion that this Constitutional Convention
was convoked and convened for the deliberate and premeditated
purpose of violating the Constitution of the United States,
the supreme law of our land, and after learning the results of
the efforts to abridge the suffrage, I am now satisfied that
that purpose bids fair to accomplish it. It only needs the
finishing touches of the administrative election officer to
launch it on its course of crime and corruption.[35]

However, this cry in the dark went unheeded. Messrs. Thom and Glass had done

their work too well. The "understanding clause," created by the future United

States Senator from the Old Dominion, was adopted.

The Suffrage Article of the New Constitution

The Constitution which emerged from this convention was a much

greater example of the historical divergence of that instrument from the

Bill of Rights, which, as usual was prefixed to the body of Virginia's organic

law. Only a casual comparison suffices to illustrate this inconsistency.

Section Six of the Declaration of Rights asserts

That all elections ought to be free; and that all
men, having sufficient evidence of permanent common interest
with, and attachment to, the community, have the right of
suffrage, and cannot be taxed, or deprived of, or damaged
in, their property for public uses, without their own
consent, or that of their representatives duly elected, or
bound by any law to which they have not, in like manner,
assented for the public good.[36]

Following this came Article II, the "Elective Franchise and

Qualifications for Office."[37] Section 18, Article II, of the new constitution provided that every male citizen of the United States, twenty-one years of age, who has been a resident of the State two years, of the county, city or town one year, and of the precinct in which he offers to vote, has paid his poll tax ($1.50) six months prior to the election, and has registered, is permitted to vote.

It was stipulated that in the registrations to be held in 1902 and 1903, of those having the qualifications of age and residence, the following could register:

> First. A person who, prior to the adoption of this Constitution served in time of war in the army or navy of the United States or of the Confederate States; or,
> Second. A son of any such person; or,
> Third. A person who owns property upon which for the year preceding that in which he offers to register, state taxes aggregating at least one dollar have been paid; or
> Fourth. A person able to read any section of this Constitution submitted to him by the officers of registration and to give a reasonable explanation of the same; or if unable to read such section, able to understand and to give a reasonable explanation thereof when read to him by the officers.[38]

The "understanding clause" thus provided a means of getting the majority of the illiterate white voters on the registration books. It was inserted to allow the "registrar to favor the white man as against the negro."[39] And it afforded an almost perfect instrument for excluding the black voter, who would find it impossible to sufficiently "understand" the constitution for the registration officials: Indeed, no one "expect (ed) an understanding clause to be administered with any degree of friendship by the white man to the suffrage of the black man...."[40]

All electors who were able and did register under the above provisions during 1902 and 1903 were "not required to register again." They remained on the registration lists permanently, unless they ceased to be residents of the State or otherwise disqualified themselves.

The Constitution specified that <u>after</u> 1902, at which time the "understanding clause" was to lose effect, every male citizen of the United States, having the qualifications of age and residence as enumerated above "shall be entitled to register, provided:

> First. That he has personally paid to the proper officer all state poll taxes assessed or assessable against him, under this or the former Constitution, <u>for the three years next preceding that in which he offers to register</u>; or, if he comes of age at such time that no poll tax shall have been assessable against him for the year preceding the year in which he offers to register, has paid one dollar and fifty cents, in satisfaction of the first year's poll tax assessable against him....[41]

In addition to paying the poll tax it was also necessary

> Second. That, unless physically unable, he make application to register in his own handwriting, without aid, suggestion or memorandum, in the presence of the registration officers, stating therein his name, age, date and place of birth, residence and occupation at the time and for the two years next preceding, and whether he has previously voted, and, if so, the state, county, and precinct in which he voted last....[42]

Next, and very significant, it was required,

> Third. That he answer on oath any and <u>all questions</u> affecting his qualifications as an elector, submitted to him by the officers of registration, which questions, and his answers thereto, shall be reduced to writing, certified by the officers, and preserved as a part of their official records.[43]

This third paragraph was cleverly conceived and worded. In requiring that each voter satisfactorily answer "all questions affecting his qualifications as an elector," a worthy successor to the "understanding clause" was provided. Therefore, at the expiration of the temporary understanding test in January, 1904, the Negro would still be at the mercy and discretion of the registrar.

Section 21 of the suffrage article specified that as a condition

of voting after January 1, 1904, only those could vote who had paid, <u>at</u>
<u>least six months prior to the election</u>, all poll taxes assessed or assessable
against them for the three years preceding that in which they offered to
vote. Again, it was required that all voters registered under either
Section 20 or 21, after January 1, 1904, would have, unless physically
unable, to "prepare and deposit their ballots without aid."[44] Any voter
registering prior to that time could secure aid in preparing his ballot
from a person of his own selection. Since most of the illiterate whites
would have ample opportunity to register by securing aid before 1904, this
educational qualification would primarily affect the Negro electorate.

Further providing for local Democratic domination, Section 30
endowed the General Assembly with the authority to

> prescribe a property qualification not exceeding two
> hundred and fifty dollars for voters in any county or
> subdivision thereof, or city or town, as a prerequisite
> for voting in any election for officers, other than the
> members of the General Assembly.[45]

The above sections constitute the basic provision for "purifying"
Virginia's elections. Although it had been claimed that the delegates were
determined to remove the fraud and corruption from the politics of the
Old Dominion, the fact is that the "understanding clause" and its successor,
which required that the elector answer all questions regarding his
qualifications, offered even greater opportunity for fraud. The morality
(or, rather casuistry) of the situation was, however, that this "fine
discrimination" was "within the letter of the law."[46] The delegates could
depart with a feeling of keen satisfaction at their successful effort to
"legalize" the defacto situation of Negro disfranchisement.

Submission or Proclamation

There was one other question with which the convention had not dis-
pensed. As their work proceeded, some of the delegates, realizing that there
was developing hostility to their work, advocated proclaiming the constitution rather than submitting it to the approval of the people. Such an attitude was completely unjustifiable as every past circumstance had indicated
that the work of the convention would be offered to a popular referendum.
The Legislature, in providing for the convention, had stipulated that the
delegates should meet "in general convention to consider, discuss, and propose
a new constitution or alterations to the existing constitution."[47] Secondly,
the Democratic Party "by every method and by all the representative utterances
through which political parties give pledges,"[48] pledged to submit the constitution. The Democrats, in their state convention of May, 1900, had adopted
a resolution written by Carter Glass,

> .... that when such Constitution shall have been framed it shall
> be submitted to a vote of the people for ratification or
> rejection....49

Thirdly, the General Assembly, in the extra session provided "for submitting
the revised and amended constitution to the people of Virginia for ratifica-
tion or rejection."[50] The act stipulated that if the convention had not completed the revision of the fundamental law in time to be voted on in the
November elections of 1901,

> It shall remain for the next general assembly to enact such
> measures as it may deem proper for submitting the revised and
> amended constitution to the people of this commonwealth for
> ratification.[51]

Again, the press of Virginia was unanimous in urging that the efforts of the
convention be passed on by the electorate.[52] In spite of this, however, the
convention entered into a prolonged debate on the issue of submission and

proclamation.[53] In April, 1902, the convention adjourned for six weeks so as

to allow the delegates to sound out public opinion on the issue.[54] Public

meetings were held in many sections as attempts were made by the Democrats to

secure a favorable opinion for proclamation.[55] It is reported that only a

hand full of people attended these so-called "mass meetings" at which senti-

ment was expressed for proclaiming the constitution.[56] They were thus in no

way valid representations of public opinion.

Notwithstanding the solemn promises and precedents, the convention

on May 29, voted 53 to 44 to proclaim the instrument in force.[57] Virginia

was presented with a new body of fundamental law. These delegates, ignoring

the fact that the convention was bound and limited in its action by the legis-

lature,[58] disdained to pursue the course which had "been generally followed

throughout the United States."[59]

In promulgating the constitution the convention ignored an almost

universal practice of referring the handiwork of constitutional conventions to

the will of the sovereign--the people. If it is true that ".... all govern-

ments derive their just power from the governed,"[60] --and who can doubt

this?--then it is almost true that the convention of 1901-02 followed an

arbitrary and dictatorial policy.

The history of state adoption of organic law had been for genera-

tions a history of popular referendum--by the electorate, either full or

limited. Since 1839, says Oberholtzer, there is

> no instance of a constitution being put into effect without
> a popular vote in any American State until Mississippi
> adopted the policy in 1890.[61]

In a pertinent statement another author writes that

> to uphold the course of the Virginia delegates it is necessary
> not merely to revive the exploded theory that the convention

is sovereign, but also to maintain that sovereignty resides in
that body, notwithstanding it was created by the people upon
the express condition that it should submit its work to them.
Such a theory seems to be without support in law, logic, or
morals.[62]

The Democrats, however, were not disposed to heed legal and consti-

tutional principles[63] as they, following the Mississippi precedent, strayed

from our basic political theory and ideal of the sovereignty of the people.

The anachronistic nature of their action, involving a positive negation of

democracy, is more apparent when it is noted that it was in Virginia that the

first judicial decision was made declaring it to be "the consent of the

people which gives validity to a constitution."[64]

The Unsuccessful Attack on the Legality of the New Constitution

The many opponents of the constitution were preparing to defeat it

when it was submitted to the approval of the people. Since this was made

impossible by the proclamation of the document, a movement was immediately

got under way to nullify the work of the convention through the courts. John

M. Wise, one of Virginia's "sons bearing an historic name," had "taken the

lead in the attempt to ... prevent the further consolidation of the oligarchy

which now rules the state."[65]

The delegates, however, cognizant of the widespread dissatisfaction

with their procedure,[66] had anticipated this move to have their efforts

voided. So, desirous of strengthening its claim to legality, the convention

had adopted the following resolution:

> Resolved, That as it has been determined to proclaim the
> constitution, provision should be made for its recognition,
> when adopted, by the political departments of the govern-
> ment, and to that end the General Assembly shall be convened
> at an early date.[67]

The Governor, on the 10th of July, took the oath to accept and

support the constitution and shortly afterwards issued a call for the legislature to convene in extra session July 15, 1902. In the meantime the executive and judicial officers of the State had qualified under the new organic
law by swearing to support it.[68] The General Assembly assembled on the
specified date and its members, with one exception, took the oath of allegiance to the new constitution.[69]

The legality of the constitution of 1902 came before the courts
for the first time in the case of Taylor v. Commonwealth.[70] Taylor, the
plaintiff, had been charged with burglary and upon arraignment pleaded guilty.
With the consent of the attorney for the Commonwealth and without the
acquiescence of the plaintiff, the county court of Augusta heard and decided
the case without a jury. Taylor was found guilty and sentenced to the
reformatory. Upon appeal to the Supreme Court of Appeals, Taylor contended
that the court had no authority to judge and sentence him without the benefit
of a jury. He alleged further that Article I, Section 8 of the constitution
of 1902, which was the authority for the court's action, was void because
the constitution had been illegally proclaimed rather than submitted to the
people.

Overruling Taylor's plea, the court held that "The Constitution of
this State... having been recognized, accepted, and acted on by the executive,
legislative, and judicial branches of the government of the State,"[71] was
valid. The court further stated that the legality of the constitution was
enhanced because "thousands of people ... throughout the state" had accepted
and registered under it. Here the court seemed to have ignored the fact that
many people had not accepted the new law. As a matter of fact a great

number of patriotic citizens of the State of Virginia, representing both the white and colored races, are now engaged in a

contest for the good of the State and for its republican form of government. Their effort is to have the new constitution declared illegal because of the manner in which it was drawn, because of its unjust discriminations in the matter of manhood suffrage, and because of its mode of promulgation.[72]

However, since the constitution was "accepted" and in force, the court refused to decide the question of the authority of the convention to proclaim it, as such a decision would have been an obiter dictum.

The next cases involving the validity of the new constitution were those of Jones, et al v. Montague,[73] and Selden, et al v. Montague,[74] which had been filed in the United States Circuit Court at Richmond in November, 1902. In the first case, Jones asked that the State Board of Canvassers be prohibited from delivering certificates of election to the delegates who had been elected to the House of Representatives in November of that year, alleging that he had been unlawfully deprived of his right to vote by the constitution of 1902. This case, together with the other one, which asked the same relief by application of an injunction, was dismissed by Chief Justice Fuller of the Circuit Court, on the grounds that the question was political, and that, therefore, the court was without jurisdiction.

The cases were brought to the Supreme Court on writs of error and the decision was handed down April 24, 1904. The court decided that

> As shown by the affidavit, and as indeed we might, perhaps take judicial notice by the presence in the House of Representatives of the individuals elected at that election from the various Congressional districts of Virginia. The thing sought to be prohibited has been done, and cannot be undone by any order of court .... The House of Representatives (which is the sole judge of the qualifications of its members) has admitted the parties holding the certificates to seats in that body, and any adjudication which this court might make would be only an ineffectual decision of the question whether or not these petitioners were wronged by what has been fully accomplished.[75]

So saying, the court, refusing to decide a "moot case,"[76] dismissed the suit.

The other case,[77] seeking injunctive relief, was dismissed on the same grounds.

Another case[78] contesting the legality of the constitution had been filed after the November elections of 1902 but was not adjudicated until 1908.[79] The plaintiff, white, had been a voter under the old constitution and could register under the new one but, failing to do so, his name was left off the new registration books and he was not allowed to vote at the election of November 4, 1902. The plaintiff contended that the new constitution was "spurious" and void because of the illegal manner in which it was framed and proclaimed.

In its decision the court[80] said that "... whether or not the restrictions and the requirements" of the "federal constitution have been duly observed in the constitutions of the states, and whether or not the states .... have observed the demands of their enabling acts, are political questions to be determined by the executive and legislative branches of the federal government."[81] Therefore, holding the issue to be political in nature, the court dismissed the case.

Very peculiar circumstances surround a case which was instituted by Edgar P. Lee, a Negro, in the United States District Court, December 13, 1902. Lee brought the suit against John S. Barbour, a member of the convention of 1901-02, and the election officials of the plaintiff's precinct, charging them with having defrauded him of his vote. He contended that the constitution was void because its creators had not taken the required oath of allegiance, because the qualifications for voting were changed and because the constitution had been illegally proclaimed. The papers of the case are on file[82] but there is no record of its having been decided. McDaniel says that:

the case appears never to have been tried.　On March 16, 1913,
Judge Waddill's stenographer wrote to the counsel for both
parties that the case would be called April 1, and unless cause
was shown to the contrary on that day, the case would be
dismissed.　John S. Wise, representing the plaintiff Lee,
returned the letter addressed him with the endorsement, "Let
her go - Dead horse."[83]

Obviously, the court, in all of these cases, had refused to decide
the real issue.　In every instance the court has avoided the vital question
of the legality of the convention and its action in proclaiming the constitution.　Therefore, the "monstrous" constitution of 1902, is the fundamental
law of the Old Dominion and as such it must remain until, as Judge Waddil
says, "it is changed, by the people of that state, or overthrown, not by the
courts, but by revolution."[84]

CHAPTER XI

VIRGINIA SINCE 1904

The effect of the new Constitution on the Virginia electorate and particularly on the black vote was immediate and pronounced. Out of a total potential vote of 447,501[1] in 1900, there were 264,095 ballots actually cast in the presidential election that year.[2] Four years later the number of votes cast in the national election shrank to 129,911[3], a decrease of 134;184. The electorate of the State had been more than cut in half!

The great majority of Negroes were disfranchised by the new constitution, as Carter Glass had predicted. Of the potential Negro voters of 1900, over half, 76,764, were illiterate.[4] Thus, in order to vote they would have to register as (1) a former soldier, or (2) the son of a former soldier, or (3) one who had paid at least a dollar in state taxes, or (4) one able to "understand and explain" the constitution. Very few Negroes could register under the soldier clauses and, as brought out at the constitutional convention, there were only 8,144 male Negroes of the State who were assessed, in 1900, for taxes on real estate valued at $300 and over.[5] Some idea of the economic plight of the colored people of Virginia is indicated by the statistics which show that in 1901 there were only 31,976 Negro men assessed with taxes on property of the value of $100, whether real, personal, or both.[6]

It is obvious, therefore, that these illiterate Negroes could only register under the "understanding clause." It is likewise obvious that few would have succeeded by that means. A good indication of the effect of the new suffrage provisions on the black vote is reflected by the Republican vote in the presidential elections of 1900 and 1904. In the former year the G.O.P.

polled 115,865 votes as compared with only 47,880 in the latter.[7] The Republican vote was diminished by almost 68,000.[8] Again, whereas in 1900 there were 147 votes cast for each thousand of the State's population, in 1904 there were only 67 votes to every thousand inhabitants.

The constitution gave the registrars great power and these men, selected by the dominant element, made it impossible for Negroes to register. Speaking of the disfranchisement of the Negroes in Virginia "by the Southern way of registering voters, " the Nation stated:

> The most preposterous questions, which no constitutional
> lawyer of eminence could answer offhand, have been asked
> of negro citizens, men of means, probity, and standing,
> when they have sought to exercise the right of suffrage
> conferred upon them by the Congress of the United States.[9]

Continuing, the Nation found that under the new constitution the number of Negro voters in the city of Manchester had been reduced from 650 to 67, in the county of Kent the number had been cut from 800 to 76, and in Middlesex County the number of colored electors had been reduced from 1,113 to 237.[10] It is no wonder, therefore, that it was found that after the registration in 1904 there were only 21,000 Negroes registered.[11] This is indeed a poor comparison with the number of registered Negro voters which in 1870 stood at 105,000.

The registrars thus found it extremely simple to exclude the masses of Negroes. The Constitution had set up adequate machinery for disfranchising the colored electorate, but "in case of doubt with a negro" who was able to "explain" the Constitution, "the registrars could always fall back on a demand for explanation of an ex-post facto law."[12]

After January 1, 1904, the three additional obstacles to voting went into effect: (1) the necessity of paying the poll tax, (2) of registering in one's own handwriting, and (3) of answering "all questions affecting" ones

"qualifications as an elector." It appears that the last section was specifically designed for the purpose of providing a written record which, if exped-
ient, could be used to disfranchise those who had passed the other tests.

The poll tax was a particularly effective instrument of disfranchisement. Its cumulative action worked a special hardship upon the poor masses,
black and white. Unless one had just come of age or had paid the tax prev-
iously, it was necessary to pay $4.50 in order to vote in 1904.[13] After the
long, ruthless fight to keep them from the polls, many Negroes naturally felt
that it was hardly worth the cost to place their ballots in the poll-boxes.
They knew that even if they voted, the whites, who were in control of the
election machinery could and would nullify their votes. Evidence of the dis-
couragement and apathy which enveloped the black electors after the convention
of 1900-02, is indicated by the figures which show that the percentage of poll
tax delinquency among Negroes increased from 47.7 per cent in 1900 to 64.6 per
cent in 1914.[14] If he could not vote, why should he pay the capitation tax
which was a prerequisite to the franchise? This was the attitude many colored
men took toward the situation. They had strenuously resisted the persistent
and relentless attack on their political rights for almost two generations and
now that the organic law had been emasculated and brought into conformity with
the designs of "white supremacy"-- since this action had been tolerated and
accepted if not justified by the Supreme Court of the United States--the black
electorate was disposed to cease its seemingly hopeless fight and "give up the
ghost."

The cause of the Negro was further hampered by the action of some of
his own leaders. Every once in a while circumstances would indicate that the
colored voter had been "sold out" by a disloyal Negro politician. It was

rumored that in the election of 1899 or 1900, John Mitchell "abdicated his political leadership and threw his support to his white associate, /Jim/ Bahne,"[15] an illiterate but powerful bar-room owner and politician in old Jackson Ward at the turn of the century. Feeling that he faced enemies both within and without, the Negro lost most of his interest in politics.

The Republicans and "Lily-Whiteism"

One of the most severe blows to the political aspirations of the Negro resulted from the increasingly hostile attitude which the Grand Old Party was assuming toward him. Having allied themselves with him and used him in the period of their struggle to consolidate the gains of industrialism, the Republicans, once their hegemony was assured, had abandoned him to his enemies of the reactionary South after 1876.[16] After the Constitutional Convention of 1901-02, the Republican party began to adopt a policy of "lily-white-ism", leaving the black voter without Frederick Douglass' ship on the political sea.

Now that the Negro was politically impotent and could no longer guarantee votes for the G.O.P., the Republicans, disdaining to campaign for his political rehabilitation, closed the doors in his face. Resentment against this policy flourished among the Negroes until in 1920 they organized a "lily-black" Republican movement and nominated an entire Negro slate for State offices and Congressmen.[17] This movement was headed by John R. Pollard, a Republican Negro attorney. The national Republican convention of 1920 had failed to seat Pollard's colored delegation and upon returning to Virginia he organized the independent "lily-black" Republicans. On this ticket John Mitchell and Maggie L. Walker ran for Governor and Lieutenant-Governor respectively, while Pollard sought election to the United States Senate. It has been said that this movement was instigated by Pollard at the behest of Democratic leaders, who desired to nullify the Negro vote by keeping it away from the Republican candidates.[18]

The "White Primary"

The most significant thing about the recent efforts of southern reactionaries to disfranchise the Negro has been the phenomenon of the "white primary." This was the instrument created by southern ingenuity after the Court, in the case of Guinn v. the United States,[19] 1915, outlawed the famous "grandfather clause." The classic example of this movement to "Nordicize" the political primary occurred in Texas in the 1920's. The first attempt, however, to exclude the Negro, was unsuccessful. The United States Supreme Court, in the case of Nixon v. Herndon,[20] decided that the act of the Texas legislature which provided that "in no event shall a negro be eligible to participate in a Democratic party primary election,"[21] was unconstitutional and void. The Court, cognizant of the fact that the Democratic primary was the determinative election in Texas and that to be barred from this is to be barred from the franchise, held that the State, in excluding Negroes from the Democratic primary, violated the 14th and 15th amendments, to the federal Constitution.

The Texas Assembly nullified the action of the Court by repealing the unconstitutional statute and passing another which was thought necessary by virtue of the "emergency" created by the Court's decision. This act provided that

> Every political party in this state through its Executive Committee shall have the power to prescribe the qualifications of its own members and shall in its own way determine who shall be qualified to vote or otherwise participate in such political party.[22]

Again the Supreme Court, in the case of Nixon v. Condon,[23] decided that this effort of the State to exclude the Negro was unconstitutional.[24] In this decision the Court found that "whatever inherent power a state political party has to determine the qualifications of its members resides in the party convention and not in any committee."[25] The Court also noted that the power exercised by the Executive Committee in this instance was not the power as a voluntary political organization but came from the State statute.[26] In consequence, the Committee's action constituted State action within the meaning of the 14th Amendment and was void.[27]

Determined to accomplish their purpose the Democrats took the tip offered by the Supreme Court and, in their state convention of May 4, 1932, passed a resolution limiting membership in the Democratic party, and thus participation in the Democratic primary, to "white citizens of the State of Texas."[28] Grovey, a colored Democrat, was restrained from voting in his party's primary by an election official. He brought suit, contending that the Democratic Convention which had adopted the restrictive measure was a creature of the State; that the primary elections were minutely regulated, that the election official was an instrument of the State; and that, therefore, the action taken by the convention and the officer constituted State action. These acts, he continued, were prohibited by the 14th and 15th amendments.

In deciding this case,[29], the Supreme Court held that although minutely regulated, the "primary is a party primary; the expenses of it are not borne by the state but by members of the party seeking nomination; "that ballots are furnished by the party, votes are counted and returns made by the party;" and that "the state recognizes the state convention as the organ of the party for the declaration of principles and the formulation of policies."[30] Not being "prepared to hold that in Texas the state convention of a party" is a "mere instrumentality.... of the state," the court reasoned that

> The state.... though it has guaranteed the liberty to organize
> political parties, may legislate for their governance when
> formed and for the method whereby they may nominate candidates,
> but must do so with full recognition of the party's right to
> exist, to define the membership, and to adopt such policies as
> it shall deem wise.[31]

Thus by means of legal technicalities and hair splitting sophistry, the Negroes of the State of Texas were forthwith disfranchised. Similarly, in other parts of the South, where the Democracy is dominant to the point of constituting a one party system, the colored electorate, denied the right to participate in the Democratic primary, is disfranchised. Nomination in the primary is tantamount to election. Since they are excluded from the primary Negroes, in voting in the general election, merely ratify the choice of the candidate selected in the primary. This, however, is not the only reason why the primaries of all political parties should be open to black members of these organizations. The privilege of participating in the nomination of a candidate for whom a qualified elector is able and expects to elect to public office is a condition inherent in the rationale of the democratic process. In the words of Professor Mechen of Chicago University:

> It is therefore true, as has often been pointed out, that the
> right to vote necessarily involves the right to nominate,
> and that the right to nominate is an essential and inseparable
> part of the right to vote. The right to nominate therefore
> becomes a constitutional right, any law which denies to the
> voter the right to determine for whom he shall vote must be
> void.[32]

The reality of this situation, however, did not impress the Justices of the Court. It is true, indeed as Chief Justice Hughes once said, that the Constitution is what the Judges say it is.

The exponents of the "white primary" in Virginia were not so fortunate as those in Texas. Seeing the situation in its true significance, a courageous Judge, in the case of West v. Bliley, et al,[33] smashed the effort to exclude the black voter from the Democratic primary in Virginia.

In their State convention of 1924, the Democrats had passed a resolution which declared that only white persons could participate in Democratic primaries. The authority for this proscriptive action was a law passed by the Virginia Legislature in 1920 which described those who might vote in a primary election as including "all persons qualified to vote at the election for which the primary is held, and not disqualified by reasons of other requirements in the law of the party to which he belongs.[34] James O. West, a Negro Democrat, was denied permission to vote in the Democratic primary held in April, 1928, to select candidates for local offices. He brought suit against the election judges, alleging that his rights guaranteed by the 14th and 15th Amendments had been abridged in pursuance of a State statute, that this constituted State action, and that the statute was thus void. The defendants entered a demurrer, alleging that the action of excluding West was a personal act, authorized by a right inherent in the political organization to which they belonged. The Judge of the District Court for the Eastern District of Virginia overruled the demurrer and continued the case on the grounds that the authority of the statute was section 36 of the constitution of Virginia, which provided that

> The General Assembly shall enact such laws as are necessary
> and proper for the purpose of securing the regularity and
> purity of general, local and primary elections....[35]

The Judge, in deciding the case, held that since the action of the State convention in limiting participation in the Democratic primaries to white persons, was pursuant to and authorized by a State statute, such action constituted State action and was therefore void. Quoting from the case of Commonwealth v. Wilcox,[36] he said:

The primary when adopted by a political party becomes an inseparable part of the election machinery, and if a candidate to be voted for at the general election is to be selected at a primary, it is impossible to secure the regularity and purity of the general election without in the first place guarding against irregularity and fraud at the primary election. The primary election constitutes a necessary part, and fulfills an essential function in the plan to promote honesty in the conduct of elections--elections which shall faithfully reflect and register the unbought will of the electors.

If there be fraud in the primary election, which is the very root from which the whole system of regulation springs, it is vain to regulate the conduct of general elections, for the fraud by which the nominee at the primary election is chosen enters into and is an inevitable constituent in the result. However fair the general election may be, if at that election men may have no choice but to vote for candidates who have been nominated by fraudulent practices at primaries, or else desert their party, which would be in most instances but to throw away their votes without achieving any good result, the effect of the election must be the consummation of a fraud and the defeat of the will of the people....[37]

The justice went to the basis of the controversy by declaring that

In the statute under consideration, there is not only a delegation of legislative power--in itself unconstitutional--but also in its purpose and effect a recognition of a further power which the legislature itself does not possess. Admittedly, the state may not provide otherwise than for equal rights and suffrage as well in the primary as in the election. This the statute does, and, if this were all there would be no ground of complaint, but it goes farther, and recognizes and enforces the right of a political party to prescribe qualifications forbidden under the Fifteenth Amendment to the Constitution of the United States. This a state may not do.[38]

In rendering his opinion, District Judge Grover stated that he was "impressed with the importance of the question raised in this case, and mindful likewise of the responsibility of its decision...."[39] He also declared that although "its effect may be to change a custom that has long obtained in the political system in effect in the State, and therefore meet with the disapproval of many, it is a consequence which, unpleasant though it may be, may nevertheless not be avoided in the performance of the duty devolving on the court."[40] On appeal to the Circuit Court of Appeals, Justice Grover's remarkable opinion was affirmed.[41]

Another legal battle was won for black suffrage in 1931 when the case of Davis v. Allen[42] was decided. Davis, a colored elector, was not allowed to register by Allen, a registrar, who alleged that the plaintiff was unable to satisfactorily answer certain questions. The action of the registrar was upheld by the lower court and Davis appealed. In its decision the Supreme Court of Appeals held that although the plaintiff obviously had little education his application for registration would have to be accepted because it had been made out in his own handwriting and poll taxes were paid. Reversing the decision of the lower court, this tribunal decided that in asking Davis "What is meant by legal residence in Virginia? When is payment of poll tax not required?" and "What are the requisites to enable one to register in Virginia?" the registrar was requiring more than that the applicant answer "questions affecting his qualifications as an elector."[43] These questions were held to be of the nature of "understanding and educational requirements" and not, therefore, sanctioned by the constitution after January 1, 1904.

The Negroes in Virginia, therefore, have won access to the Democratic primary and, since the abortive independent "lily-white" movement of 1920-21, have made extensive use of this right.[44] This march away from the Republican standard has been encouraged by many Negro leaders[45] who contend that a diversion of colored ballots to the Democracy would give rise to a "new respect to the Negro vote."[46] Obviously the Negro, in voting in the Democratic primary, is forced to choose men rather than programs. Consequently the value of this right is doubtful since "frequently the candidates are all strictly conservative....."[47]

CHAPTER XII

CONCLUSION

The long struggle to eliminate the Negro voter from Virginia politics has had at least three profound effects on the general political condition of the State. In the first place, the Negro has been reduced to a position of political impotence. In 1867 there were more than 105,000 registered colored voters in Virginia. By 1904, however, the number had been reduced to less than 25,000. Cleverly linking the slogan of "unlimited suffrage" with "universal amnesty," the old leadership returned to power in 1869. The freedmen were offered the olive branch in return for their political support. Failing to secure the Negro ballots, the whites began a movement to nullify his vote. The Democrats were in control of the election machinery and thus were usually able to insure the triumph of their candidates. In the early 1870's the Democrats placed additional impediments in the path of the Negro by amending the constitution. Thus between 1872 and 1879 the black elector was of minor importance in the politics of the Old Dominion.

The Readjusters came upon the scene in 1879 and the Negro vote again became extremely important. Disaffection in white ranks placed the colored voter in a strategic position. Realizing that the Negro was the chief factor in this class movement, the old leaders intensified the attack on the colored electorate. Every conceivable weapon was used to destroy the prestige and power which the Negro achieved during "Readjusterism." Upon their return to control in 1884, the reactionaries re-enforced fraud and corruption with intimidation and coercion. Mob violence and lynchings increased considerably after the election of John Langston, the only Negro ever to represent Virginia in Congress. Following this period of corruption and violence, the whites returned to the practice of excluding the Negro by means of legislative enactment. Most important of these measures passed in the interest of "white supremacy" were the Anderson-McCormick law of 1884 and the Walton Act of 1894. The legislative attack on the black electorate was culminated in the special constitutional convention of 1901-1902, which was held to legalize the defacto condition of Negro disfranchisement. Overwhelmed by this ruthless assault on what, theoretically, were their constitutional rights, the Negroes of Virginia settled into a state of political apathy and dejection.

In the middle of the 1920's the colored electors followed the advice of their leaders and went into the Democratic primary elections in an effort to make the best use of their limited vote. The leaders of the Democracy immediately attempted to prevent this by instituting the "white primary". Although the Court, contrary to its usual course, blocked this move, access to the Democratic primary did not materially change the condition of the Negro. The degree to which the Negro participates in local government is indicated by the fact that in Richmond, where his participation in Virginia politics has always been greatest, there were only 4,933 colored registered electors out of a total of 48,470 registered voters in 1925.[2] This means that the Negro, even though he comprised over 31 per cent of the population of the City in 1920, had only 10 per cent of the voters. The author, in his investigation of conditions in Richmond during the past year, found that any change in the situation since the early '20's has been only for the worse. Today, out of 24,000 to 25,000 potential Negro voters[3], there are hardly more than 1,800 registered colored eledtors in the City.[4]   Of these

1,800 elegible voters, not more than 1,200 or 1,300 actually voted in the

last election. It is believed that this discrepancy was due to the failure

of many old-line Republicans to go to the trouble of voting in the final

election which had already been determined in the Democratic primary, the

absence of many qualified electors from the City, and a general lack of

interest.[5] The situation in Richmond symbolizes the fact that the 650,185

colored people who, in 1930, constituted 26.8 per cent of the population

of Virginia, have no effective voice in the formulation and administration

of the laws under which they live.

     Secondly, the movement to bar the Negro from Virginia politics has

not been devoid of repercussions in the white electorate. The same weapons,

legal and illegal, which were used to nullify the Negro vote have often been

utilized to offset white ballots. This has been particularly true in ex-

cluding the poor white Republicans of the western sections. A prominent

local member of the G. O. P. states that there are more whites unable to vote

in Virginia than Negroes.[6] The poll tax is as much of a deterrent to the

exercise of suffrage among the poor whites as it is among the Negroes. In

1920 there was a population of 2,309,187 in Virginia but only 231,001 votes

were cast in the presidential election of that year,[7] that is, one person out

of ten voted. In the gubernatorial election the following year it was even

worse. Only one out of eleven voted.[8] In polling a total vote of 229,777[9]

in the Congressional elections of 1924, Virginia cast only 17.9 per cent of

her total potential vote.[10] This compares very unfavorably with her sister

states, West Virginia and Kentucky. The former cast 76.99 per cent of her

potential vote and the latter, 62.5 per cent." The Richmond News-Leader has

estimated that in 1916 and 1920 only 4 per cent of the total population of that city elected the mayor.[12] After the electorate has been theoretically doubled by extension of the suffrage to women, the local officials were elected in 1924 by only 5 per cent of Richmond's population.[13] This, as noted by the News-Leader, is indeed a poor example of American "democracy."

Recent statistics further illustrate the failure of democratic processes to function in Virginia. In the presidential election of 1936, the percentages of eligible white electors who cast ballots in the seven southern states were as follows: South Carolina, 13 per cent; Alabama and Georgia, 19 per cent; Arkansas, 17 per cent; Mississippi, 16 per cent; Texas, 25 per cent, and Virginia, 31 per cent.[14] When it is realized that the average vote for the country as a whole in this election was 62 per cent,[15] these figures take on added significance. Again, the Old Dominion only polled an average of 33,449 votes in electing each of her 10 Congressmen in 1936 as compared with the 112,998 votes Minnesota cast for each of her 10 Congressmen.[16] The average for the entire nation was 98,099 per Congressman.[17] Being excluded from the franchise, the black and white masses of Virginia, and to a greater extent those in other sections of the South, are unable to exert effective political pressure upon southern politicians and, therefore, cannot greatly influence their Congressmen on national issues. The President of the United States recently called attention to this situation in a speech made at Gainesville, Georgia, in which he vigorously attacked "the feudal system" of the South.[18]

The third effect of the continuous struggle to submerge the black voter is the establishment and maintenance of "race politics" at the expense of the economic advancement of the community. This condition began in the days immediately after the Civil War and continues unmitigated today. It is important to remember that Conservatism, which was collateral with "white politics" prior to the adoption of the name "Democrat" in the 80's, denoted something more than a political party. It was a state of mind of the dominant white aristocrats who elaborated it into a social code. And this attitude upon adoption by the poor whites was exaggerated and carried to fanatical heights. Although the security of the "Bourbon" had been seriously weakened by the collapse of the slave system, they never lost their prestige and were determined to reestablish their former control. The historic conflict between the aristocrats and the lower classes, the latter of which represented the democratic forces was compromised and finally resolved by the union of both classes of whites into solidarity against the blacks. It was the use of this method of playing race against race that enabled the reactionaries to check the indigenous liberalizing movement which arose after the Civil War. The radicalism which had waxed strong during the period of Reconstruction and the Readjuster triumph of 1879-18, was an essentially democratic revolt against Conservative domination. Although forced to make concessions to liberalism, Conservatism prevented the realization of the revolutionary significance of the Civil War.

"Readjusterism," the most significant episode in Virginia's political history, 1870-1900, differed from the radicalism of Reconstruction only in that the latter received considerable stimulus from outside influences, while the former was a purely indigenous movement. The collaboration between the lower classes of whites and blacks contained the possibility of a democratic resurgence which was destined to carry through the aborted reforms of Reconstruction. However, the cohesion and stability of this bi-racial movement foundered on the shoals of racial antagonism, the bulwark of reactionary control. This political alignment on the basis of race has been effectively maintained although frequently threatened. It is only now beginning to crack.

The maintenance of the one party system in the South, with the tremendous handicaps which inevitably go with it, has drawn sporadic internal criticism. As early as 1900 the Governor of West Virginia, William A MacCorkle, saw in the "demand of this industrial regeneration" of the South the necessity of bringing about the "absolute settlement of political complexities."[19] If the South was to grasp the opportunities presented by steady industrial and financial progress, Governor MacCorkle said, the whites cannot continue to devote themselves "to the one and sole idea of holding ourselves solid on the Negro question.... The tyranny of the solid vote to be maintained on the question is the most burdensome and exhausting which ever afflicted a people."[20]

This policy of racial separation has not been confined to the political arena. It extends to every phase of life in Virginia. In the first place discrimination against and segregation of the Negro is sanctioned and enforced by the law. Since 1902 colored people have been forced to travel in separate railway coaches.[21] In 1912 the Virginia Legislature, contending that "the preservation of public morals, public health and public order, in the cities and towns of this commonwealth is endangered by the residence of white and colored people in close proximity to one another," provided for the division of cities into "white" and "colored districts."[22] In 1926 a law was passed requiring that white and colored persons be separated in "all public halls, theatres, opera houses, motion picture shows and places of public entertainment and public assemblages."[23] In this connection, it is interesting to note that Virginia has recently changed her legal definition of "Negro." At one time any one having one-twelfth Negro blood was considered colored. Next, any one with one-sixteenth Negro blood was put into this category. In 1930 the legislature provided that "Every person in whom there is any Negro blood shall be deemed and taken to be a colored person."[24]

In addition to the legal structure for enforcing segregation, Virginia has evolved another method which, though subtler, is no less effective in keeping the races apart. This is the policy of encouraging and even sponsoring the development of Negro institutions separate from although dependent upon, those of the whites. White leaders think that the "race problem" is solved by keeping interracial contacts at an absolute minimum. They therefore encourage and help the Negroes to organize and maintain black banks, and black insurance companies, and to duplicate as far as possible the white institutions and values. In describing the function of this policy of racial separatism, Dr. Abram L. Harris states:

> This institutional duplication which takes place behind the walls of segregation is not only profitable to the ambitious members of the Negro middle class, but, in serving the social needs of the black community, it reduces public contact between the whites and Negroes and makes possible the development of black respectability on the basis of the prevailing social values of the surrounding white community.[25]

This policy of "racial parallelism" in Virginia serves to keep the Negro "in his place" and, at the same time, yields compensatory benefits to the Negro leaders.

Deplorable as conditions are in Virginia, they are not as bad as in some other sections of the South. Many of the old leaders have gone from the scene and the opinion was expressed by many that the passing of Carter Glass will mark the belated end of the virilent anti-Negro era. A number of local people believe that today the Negroes face a much more encouraging political future. They are convinced that many of them can vote if they try. However, it is also true, as disclosed in a survey by the United States Department of Labor, that "the inability to pay the poll tax is a major factor"[26] in the disfranchisement of many workers and farmers. Although prohibited after 1903, the "understanding clause" has frequently been used.[27] Lewinson writes that ".... in Hampton at least, examinations of this sort were still being conducted in 1929-30...."[28]

Possibly indicative of a change for the better in the Old Dominion is the attitude of a Virginia writer, an ex-mayor, and commonwealth's attorney, who is willing that "in the settlement of the respective political rights of the two races in the Southern States," each should have a "proper share of the representatives in Congress from that section."[29] However, this concession to the black voter is to be made only on condition that the white representatives be elected by an "exclusively white electorate" and the colored representatives by "negro voters alone."[30] Further, Gravely believes that in each southern State there should be a "Negro assembly" which, while having "the privilege of initiating, discussing, and reviewing legislation," should be, however, "without any voting power in connection therewith."[31] Leaving this extension of racial parallelism into the political sphere, it is interesting to note that the Richmond News-Leader, a liberal local paper, has kept up a constant campaign for the last several years in an attempt to encourage greater interest in politics and general political reform. Each year this paper awards scrolls of merit to those who have come of age during the past year and have registered.[32]

Although not so flagrant as in some other parts of the country, the Negro in Virginia is still proscribed in the exercise of his basic rights. The rigidity of the legal and social structure there makes for the degredation of the black man and, in doing so, also degrades the lower class whites. It is in these elements that rest the possibilities of instituting a progressive reorientation of Virginia politics. It is they who must establish a rational political alignment and enter into a joint struggle for economic and social reform. Any successful movement in this direction cannot of course

forego persistent and wholehearted political participation. For economic,

social and political rights are not found in separate and distinct categories;

they are inseparably bound together and indispensable to one another. If a

people desire one, they want the others, and if they obtain one they must

secure the others. As in the time of Booker Washington and more so today,

political power is a vital and essential correlative of economic security.

FOOTNOTES

Chapter I

1. In 1880 the Negroes still constituted 60.7 per cent of the population of South Carolina. Census Reports. 1880.

2. United States Census Reports, 1870, Vol. XI, XII.

3. Allen, G. L., The Negro Question in the United States, pp. 34-36.

4. After noting the highly satisfactory manner in which the military had helped to conduct an election, a local newspaper was moved to say that "The 'boys in blue' are decidedly popular in this city." The Richmond Whit, Oct. 24, 1867.

Chapter II

1. Ambler, G. H. Sectionalism in Virginia, 1776-1861, pp. 170-172.

2. Eckenrode, H. J., The Political History of Virginia During Reconstruction, p. 10; McDaniel, R. C., The Virginia Constitutional Convention of 1901-02, p. 3.

3. Appleton's Annual Cyclopaedia, 1865, p. 816.

4. During 1861-65, Virginia thus had two governments. However, Pierpont's administration, after the creation of West Virginia, embraced only a few counties. Appleton's Annual Cyclopaedia, 1865, p. 816.

5. A constitutional convention had been called by the Alexandria government in May 1864, at which time a constitution for the loyal section of the state was drawn up. Eckenrode, op. cit., p. 30; Morton, R.L. The Negro in Virginia Politics, 1865-1902, p. 15.

6. Eckenrode, op. cit., p. 30. The other rebel states were being put under provisional governments and there was the beginning of a movement to extend the suffrage to the Negro.

7. The Richmond Times, July 26, 1865.

8. Reports of the Committee, 39th Congress, 1st Session, Part II, pp. 10-11.

9. Alexandria Gazette, June 13, 1865, as quoted in Eckenrode, op. cit., p. 33.

10. Eckenrode, op.cit., pp. 33-34.

11. Johnson, a man of the lower strata of southern pre-war society, had continued a modified form of Lincoln's "mild" policy of reconstruction.

12. See Hacker and Kendricks, History of the United States Since 1865; Beard, C.A., and M., The Rise of American Civilization; Lewison, P., Race, Class and Party; DuBois, W.E.R., Black Reconstruction, and, highly partisan, Bowers, C. The Tragic Era.

13. Appleton's Annual Cyclopaedia, 1865, p. 818.

14. Beale, H. K., The Critical Year, pp. 191-93.

15. Lewinson, P., Race, Class, and Party, p. 32.

16. Ibid., p. 31-32.

17. Acts of Assembly, 1865-66, p. 91.

18. Appleton's Annual Cyclopaedia, 1865, p. 818.

19. Eckenrode says of the vagrancy law that although it was "probably justified by the economic necessity of the time.... it was most unpolitic.... It seemed to savor of slavery," op.cit., p. 42.

20. Appleton's Annual Cyclopaedia, 1865, p. 818.

21. Ibid., 18 6, p. 819.

22. The party was called the "Union Republican Party of Virginia," Morton, The Negro in Virginia Politics, p. 23, and Eckenrode, op.cit., p. 47.

23. The National Republican Convention, meeting at Philadelpha in 1866, adopted "manhood" suffrage. J. W. Hunnicut and George Tucker, white Virginiana, led the fight for unlimited suffrage. Eckenrode, op.cit., p. 49; Morton, op.cit. p. 25.

24. The Enquirer, April 17, 18, 1866.

25. Senate Documents, 39th Congress, 2nd Session, Vol. 2, No. XXIX, p. 17; Appleton's Annual Cyclopaedia, 1866, p. 765.

26. Ibid.

27. The Enquirer, Dec. 5, 1866.

28. Appleton's Annual Cyclopaedia, 1866, p. 765.

29. The Enquirer, January 10, 1867.

30. Hacker and Kendrick, op. cit., p. 23.

31. Eckenrode, op. cit., p. 52.

32. Ibid.

CHAPTER III

1. Hacker, L.M. and Kendrick, B.B., The United States Since 1865, p. 23.

2. Chandler, J.A.C., The History of Suffrage in Virginia, p. 50.

3. Documents of the Constitutional Convention, 1867-68, pp. 52, 56.

4. Eckenrode, op.cit., p. 83.

5. Taylor, A.A., The Negro in the Reconstruction of Virginia, p. 221.

6. However, the election was not actually begun until Oct. 22, 1867; Appleton's Annual Cyclopaedia, 1867, p. 763.

7. Eckenrode, op. cit., p. 48.

8. Ibid., pp. 76, 77; Chandler, op. cit., pp. 35-38.

9. The Whig, Oct. 17, 1867.

10. The Richmond Dispatch, April 19, 1867.

11. Ibid.

12. Eckenrode, op. cit., pp. 67-76. These men were Marmaduke Johnson, Raleigh F. Daniel, and W. H. Farland. The Dispatch, April 15, 16, 1867.

13. Appleton's Annual Cyclopaedia, 1867, p. 759.

14. Such radical accommodation--acceptance of inferior and superior racial positions--was essential to the stability of the institution of slavery and to the physical well-being of the slaves and, to a lesser degree, the masters. Force, as an active instrument of coercion, was only used in an emergency, being kept in the background until an unusual situation arose. And here it would seem, the institution meets its most severe indictment; forcing a people to accept a status, and, in time, an attitude of inferiority.

15. The Whig, Oct. 17, 18, 19, 1867.

16. Ibid.

17. This was the name adopted by native white partisans. The movement, however, was reactionary rather than conservative.

18. The Enquirer, July 2, 1867; Eckenrode, op. cit., p. 49.

19. Taylor, op. cit., p. 213.

20. The Enquirer and Examiner, Oct. 21, 1867.

169

21. *Ibid.*, Oct. 22, 1867. This editorial was entitled: "How to Avert a War of Races /!/"

22. The Whig, Oct. 19, 1867.

23. The Enquirer and Examiner, Oct. 23, 1867.

24. Documents of the Convention, 1867-68, pp, 52.56.

25. *Ibid.*

26. *Ibid.*; 8,345 Negroes failed to vote. Appleton's Annual Cyclopaedia, 1867. p. 763.

27. Almost 15,000 whites voted in favor of it.

28. The Whig, Oct. 30, 1867.

29. The Enquirer, Nov. 1, 1867.

30. Eckenrode, *op. cit.*, p. 56.

31. Eckenrode, *op. cit.*, p. 76.

32. The Whig, October 25, 1767.

33. Taylor, *op.cit.*, p. 224.

34. The Enquirer and Examiner, Nov. 1, 1867.

35. Eckenrode, *op.cit.*, p. 87.

36. The Enquirer and Examiner, Oct. 26, 1867, quoting from the Lynchburg News.

37. The Whig, Oct. 30, Nov. 1, 2, 1867.

38. Appleton's Annual Cyclopaedia, 1867, p. 763.

39. Eckenrode, *op.cit.*, pp.85-86.

40. The Enquirer and Examiner, December 12, 1867.

41. *Ibid.*, Oct. 26, 1867.

42. Morton, The Negro in Virginia...., p. 50.

43. The Whig, October 28, 1867.

44. *Ibid.*, quoting from the Lynchburg Virginian.

CHAPTER IV

1. Debates and Proceedings of the Constitutional Convention, 1867-1869, pp. 5,6.

2. Taylor says of Bayne: ... he was quick on his feet, and he generally spoke to the point. An orator by nature, too, he was more than a match for his opponents..." op.cit., p.238.

3. The Dispatch and The Enquirer, Jan. 10, 18, 24, 1868.

4. Debates, pp. 140-205.

5. Article X, Constitution of 1868.

6. Snavely, T. R., The Taxation of Negroes in Virginia, pp. 6, 8.

7. Article VIII, this was Virginia's first public school system.

8. Taylor, op. cit., p. 241.

9. Article IV.

10. These were the disfranchising clause and the so-called "iron-Clad oath."

11. The Enquirer and Examiner, Dec. 5, 11, 1867.

12. Morton, The Negro in Virginia.... pp. 64-65.

13. Appleton's Annual Cyclopaedia, 1868, Va., p. 761.

14. A. H. H. Stuart complained that "apathy seemed to pervade the State and everybody remained quiescent," Taylor, op.cit., p. 247.

15. Stuart, A.H.H., The Restoration of Virginia, pp. 27-29. It was said General Stoneman, who had succeeded General Schofield as commander of the Republican area, favored this plan.

16. Morton, op.cit., p. 66.

17. The Whig, January 5, 6, 7, 1869.

18. Braxton, A.C., The Fifteenth Amendment, p. 52.

19. Stuart, op.cit., p. 28.

20. The National Intelligencer, Jan. 16, 1869.

21. Ibid. The New York Herald (Republican) was quite favorable to the "new movement."

22. Ibid.

23. Appleton's Annual Cyclopaedia, 1869, p. 709.

24. The Code of Virginia, 1873, p. 26.

25. This Committee was headed by Governor H. H. Wells and contained some Negroes, Taylor, op.cit., p. 249.

26. Appleton's Annual Cyclopaedia, 1869, p. 713.

27. The Enquirer, May 27, 29, 1869. The Whig, May 4, 8, 1869.

28. The Whig, May 30, July 5, 1869.

29. Ibid., July 6, 1869.

30. Ibid., May 4; June 27, 28, 1869. In spite of the subservient demands made by the whites, they were always able to count on some black ballots, however small the number might be.

31. Morton, The Negro in Virginia...., p. 75.

32. Lewison, op.cit., pp. 54-60.

33. Eckenrode quotes an interesting definition of the Union League which, it was said, was organized "as an aid to the effective carrying out of the humane objects and purposes of those in the North who believed that the ballot in the hands of the negro would be preferable to bullets in the muskets of a standing army which would have been necessary for an indefinite period in many sections of the South." Op.cit., p.61.

34. In South Carolina the situation was vastly different and there the Union League functioned as the guiding spirit in the revolutionary "dictatorship" set up during Reconstruction. For an excellent discussion, see Allen, R.S., Reconstruction, the Battle for Democracy.

35. The Enquirer, Oct. 31, 1867.

36. Appleton's Annual Cyclopaedia, 1869, p. 713.

37. Ibid.

38. Ibid.

39. Ibid.

40. Ibid.

41. Ibid.

42. Stuart, op.cit., pp. 56-57.

43. The Whig, July 9, 1869.

44. Ibid., July 8, 1869.

45. Taylor, op.cit., p. 257.

46. The Whig, July 7, 8, 1869.

47. This was the figure at which the Negro vote in this election was set.

48. Eckenrode, op.cit., pp. 73-74.

49. Appleton's Annual Cyclopaedia, 1869, p. 714.

50. Ibid., Nov. 26, 1869.

51. Ibid.

52. The Whig, Nov.26, 1869. This was a minority report.

53. The Whig, Nov. 26, 1869.

54. Appleton's Annual Cyclopaedia, 1869, p. 715.

55. G. C. Walker, the successful Conservative candidate, had acted as pro-
    visional governor since the resignation of Wells on September 21, 1869.

56. The Enquirer, Oct. 9, 1869.

CHAPTER V

1. The Dispatch, July 11, 1870.

2. Ibid.

3. Ibid., April 1, 1871.

4. Appleton's Annual Cyclopaedia, 1871, p. 766.

5. Morton, The Negro in Virginia..., op.,cit., p. 87.

6. The Nation, Vol. 17, No. 436, Nov. 6, 1873.

7. South Carolina, Miss., etc.

8. Morton, The Negro in Virginia.... p. 89

9. Taylor, op.cit. p. 266.

10. Sheldon, W. D., Populism in the Old Dominion, p. 13.

11. Douglass, Frederick, U. S. Grant and the Colored people (speech)

12. Taylor, op. cit., p. 269.

13. The Dispatch, September 14, 1874.

14. The Dispatch, October 25, 26, 1872.

15. Acts of Assembly, 1871, pp. 226-229.

16. Southeastern sections having heavy Negro majorities.

17. Chandler, J.A.C., Representation in Virginia, p. 82.

18. The Richmond Planet, Nov. 24, 1932.

19. The Constitutional Convention of 1867-68 had broadened the basis of
    popular participation in local government and increased the number of
    offices in order to prevent control from being secured and wielded by
    a few reactionary families, as had happened in the past.

20. Acts of Assembly, 1874, pp. 208-12.

21. The Dispatch, Nov. 7, 10, 1874.

22. Taylor, op.cit., p. 267.

23. Acts of Assembly, 1874-75, pp. 200-203. The Legislature, in 1870, had
    assessed all men over 21 years of age with a poll tax of one dollar
    which, by sections one and five, Art. X, of the constitution of 1868,
    was to "be applied exclusively in aid of public free schools."

24. Acts of Assembly, 1875-76, p. 83.

25. The Dispatch, Feb. 28, 1880.

26. Acts of Assembly, 1874-75, pp. 200-203.

27. The other disqualifying crimes were: bribery at elections, embezzlement
    of public funds, duelling, treason, and felony. Art. III, Consti-
    tution of 1868.

28. Acts of Assembly, 1875-76, pp. 82-87.

29. McDaniel, op.cit., p. 6.

30. Acts of Assembly, 1874-75, p. 202.

31. Ibid., p. 401.

32. Ibid.

33. Acts of Assembly, 1874-75, p. 402.

34. The vote was 129,373 for and 98,559 against the amendments. Appleton's
    Annual Cyclopaedia, 1876, p. 800.

35. Acts of Assembly, 1876-77, p. 280-281.

36. Snavely, op.cit., p. 19.

37. In the Richmond Planet of Nov. 24, 1932, Mr. B. P. Vandervall, one of Richmond's old time Negro politicians, gives an interesting description of the political interest of the colored people of Virginia in the latter part of the last century.

38. Snavely, op. cit., pp. 15-16.

39. McDaniel, op.cit., p. 6.

40. Morton, The Negro in Virginia..., p. 93.

41. The Richmond State, as quoted in Snavely, op.cit., pp. 19-20.

42. Appleton's Annual Cyclopaedia, 1875, p. 751.

43. Ibid.

44. Ibid.

45. The Dispatch, Aug. 29, 30, 1872.

46. The Whig, Oct. 17, 1867; The Dispatch, Apr. 23, 1872.

47. The Dispatch, May 9, 1867, April 23, 1872.

48. Hacker and Kendrick, op.cit., p. 54.

49. Lewinson, op.cit., pp. 75-92.

50. Appleton's Annual Cyclopaedia, 1872, pp. 140-154.

CHAPTER VI

1. Pearson, C. C., The Readjuster Movement in Virginia, pp. 5-12.

2. Ibid., pp. 17-19.

3. The Whig, Feb. 26, 1879.

4. Pearson, op.cit., p. 66.

5. Ibid., p. 62.

6. Ibid.

7. Ibid., p. 177.

8. Whig, Nov. 1, 1880.

9. Dispatch, Feb. 27, 28, 1879.

10. Morton, The Negro in Va...., p. 103.

11. Pearson, op.cit., pp. 10-14.

12. Dispatch, Nov. 10, 1879; Morton, History of Virginia, p. 196.

13. Six Negro Republicans were elected to the Assembly. Appleton's Annual
    Cyclopaedia, 1879, p. 344.

14. Morton, op.cit., p. 196.

15. The Funders had found it necessary to place a few Negro nominees in the
    race.

16. McDaniel, op.cit., p. 7.

17. The Dispatch, Nov. 8, 1879.

18. Ibid., Nov. 10, 1879.

19. The Whig, Nov. 2, 1881; Oct. 26, 1883.

20. McDaniel, op.cit., pp. 6-7.

21. Appleton's Annual Cyclopaedia, 1881, p. 780.

22. Morton, History of Virginia., p. 209.

23. McDaniel, op.cit., pp. 8-9; Ibid., p. 209.

24. Dispatch, Nov. 11, 13, 1879.

25. Ibid., Nov. 10, 1879.

26. Ibid., Nov. 13, 1881.

27. Ibid., Nov. 13, 1879.

28. Taylor, op.cit., p. 281.

29. 13th, 14th, and 15th Amendments.

30. Many colored schools had been closed. Appleton's Annual Cyclopaedia,
    1885. p. 778: "There was in 1883-84 a school for every 70 white child-
    ren, but only one for every 128 colored."

31. Ibid., p. 283.

32. The Whig, Feb. 18, 1835.

33. Taylor, op.cit., p. 282.

34. Ibid., p. 282.

35. Acts of Assembly, 1879-1880.

36. *Ibid*., 1881-1882, pp. 213-214.

37. Snavely, *op.cit*., p. 20.

38. *Ibid*.

39. The Richmond State, quoted in Snavely, pp. 19-20.

40. Taylor, *op.cit*., p. 283.

41. Acts of Assembly, 1879-1880, pp. 81-82, 87.

42. The Whig, Feb. 18, 19, 1885.

43. *Ibid*., Feb. 18, 1885.

44. Pearson, *op.cit*., p. 5.

45. *Ibid*., pp. 5-6.

46. The Whig, July 24, 1883.

47. The Dispatch, November 1, 3, 1883, November 4, 1884.

48. *Ibid*., Oct. 26, 1883.

49. The Whig, Feb. 24, 1885.

50. *Ibid*., Feb. 25, 26, 1885.

51. The Dispatch, Nov. 4, 1883.

52. Morton, *The Negro in Virginia*...., p. 119.

53. Appleton's Annual Cyclopaedia, 1883, p. 816.

54. The Whig, Feb. 25, 1885.

55. *Ibid*., Feb. 25, 1885.

56. *Ibid*.

57. Taylor, *op.cit*., p. 268.

58. The Whig, Feb. 25, 1885.

59. *Ibid*., March 2, 1885.

60. The Dispatch, Nov. 2, 4, 1883.

61. Pearson, *op.cit*., pp. 149-51.

62. The Dispatch, Nov. 10, 14, 1883.

63. Ibid.

64. Morton, The History of Virginia...., p. 209.

65. McDaniel, op.cit., p. 8.

66. Acts of Assembly, 1883-84, p. 150.

67. Ibid., p. 151.

68. Appleton's Annual Cyclopaedia, 1884, p. 797.

69. Acts of Assembly, 1884, pp. 146-151.

70. Appleton's Annual Cyclopaedia, 1885, p. 797.

71. Acts of Assembly, 1884, pp. 152-153.

72. The Whig, March 2, 1885, compiled in "The Campaign of 1887."

73. The Times, Feb. 10, 12, 1894.

74. Ibid., Feb. 12, 13, 1394.

75. The Dispatch, Feb. 24, 1894.

CHAPTER VII

1. Pearson, op.cit., pp. 202-08.

2. Sheldon, W.D., Populism in the Old Dominion, p. 52.

3. The Planet was and still is published in Richmond.

4. Harris, The Negro as Capitalist, p. 74.

5. Ibid.

6. Appleton's Annual Cyclopaedia, 1895, p. 896.

7. Ibid.

8. The Dispatch, April 11, 1884.

9. Morton, The Negro in Virginia... p. 123.

10. The Times, as quoted in The Dispatch, Feb. 13, 1894.

11. Dunning, The Undoing of Reconstruction, Atlantic Monthly, Vol. 88, Oct. 1901, pp. 443-44.

12. The Dispatch, Jan. 2, 1889; The Times, Nov. 1, 3, 1884.

13. The Readjusters and Republicans held a "Coalition" convention in 1884 and the name "Republican" was officially adopted.

14. The Dispatch, Nov. 4, 1885.

15. Gravely, W.H., _Can the Water be Made Fine?_ p. 21.

16. Langston, J. M., _From Virginia Plantation to the National Capital_, p.445.

17. Lewinson, pp. 56-58; McDaniel, _op.cit._, p. 26.

18. Dunning, _op.cit._, pp. 444-45.

19. McDaniel, _op.cit._, p. 27.

20. Interview at Richmond.

21. Dispatch, November 1, 1888.

22. _Ibid._

23. McDaniel, _op.cit._, p. 27.

24. Dispatch, Feb. 20, 1894.

25. The Times, Feb. 19, 22, 1894.

26. The Dispatch, Feb. 2, 1894.

27. _Ibid._

28. Ibid.

29. The Times, Feb. 19, 22, 1894.

30. McDaniel, _op.cit._, p. 28

31. Sheldon, _op.cit._, p. 54.

32. Morton, _The Negro in Virginia_...., p. 129.

33. Sheldon, _op.cit._, p. 55.

34. _Ibid._, p. 129.

35. Langston, _op.cit._, p. 445.

36. Part of the "Black Belt."

37. Morton says of him: "Langston was a Virginia mulatto, who had been educated at the North, where he lived until he came to Petersburg, Va., as a teacher. He was unscrupulous although intelligent and fluent." _Negro in Va_..... p. 127.

38. Langston, op.cit., p. 444.

39. Ibid., p. 445.

40. Ibid.

41. Langston was quite bitter about this "cunning, false and base" action on the part of Douglass. Langston, op.cit., p. 467.

42. The Dispatch, Nov. 1, 1888.

43. Ibid.

44. Langston, op. cit., p. 478.

45. The Dispatch, Oct. 23, 1888.

46. Ibid., Nov. 4, 1883.

47. U. S. Contested election case, Langston v. Venable, 51st Congress, p.1455.

48. Ibid., pp. 1453-59; Langston, op.cit., p.480.

49. The Dispatch, Oct. 29, 1888, Nov. 2, 4, 5, 1888.

50. Morton, The Negro in Virginia, p. 125.

51. Ibid., p. 136.

52. Journals of the Senate and House, 1897-1898, pp. 16-17.

53. Ibid., p. 17.

54. The Dispatch, Feb. 2, 1894.

55. Morton says that "the number of rapings by Negro men were increasing at an alarming rate.... Records of the charges show that the lynchings were the result of the Nature of the crime rather than race prejudice." The Negro in Virginia... p. 136-37.

56. The Dispatch, Feb. 25, 1894.

57. Ibid.

CHAPTER VIII

1. Hicks, John D., The Populist Revolt, pp. 275-289.

2. Hacker and Kendrick, op.cit., pp. 183-86.

3. Sheldon, op.cit., pp. 7-8.

4. Census of 1890, House Reports, 52nd Congress, 1st Session, Vol. 50.

5. Sheldon, op.cit., p. 31.

6. The Dispatch, October 7, 1890.

7. Ibid., November 1, 3, 1892.

180

8. _Ibid._, Oct. 24, 27, 30, 1893.

9. Sheldon, _op.cit._, p. 101.

10. _Ibid._, p. 92.

11. The Dispatch, Aug. 25, 1392.

12. Only 13 Populists were elected to the General Assembly, 10 of whom were from the Southside--Black Belt district, Morton, _The Negro in Va._,_op. cit._, p. 132; Sheldon, _op.cit._, p.104.

13. The Populists had collaborated with the local Republicans and captured the legislatures of S.C., Ala., Md., and Ga. Populist governors had been elected in Ga., S.C., and Tenn. plus several Congressmen, Morton, _The Negro in Va._...., pp. 132-133.

14. Contested election case,Goode v.Epes,53rd Congress,3rd Sess.V.2,1895,p. 25, 120.

15. Sheldon, _op.cit._, p. 92.

16. _Ibid._, p. 92.

17. _Ibid._, p. 63.

18. Excerpt from speech of candidate Field, The Dispatch, July 21, 1892.

19. The Dispatch, Jan. 9, 1894.

20. The Times, Dec. 20, 21, 1893; Jan. 3, 6, 7, 1894.

21. The Dispatch, Jan. 2, 1889.

22. _Ibid._, Dec. 17-19, 1893.

23. Contested Election Case, Goode v. Epes, House Reports, 53rd Congress, Vol. 2, No. 1952, 1893-95, pp. 25, 38, 120.

24. The Virginia Sun, June 14, 1893.

25. Morton, R. L., _History of Virginia_, p. 299.

26. The Dispatch, Jan. 1, 1894.

27. _Ibid._, Feb. 28, 1894.

28. _Ibid._, Mar. 3, 1894.

29. _Ibid._, Mar. 3, 1894.

30. _Ibid._

31. Acts of Assembly, 1893-94, p. 862.

32. Acts of Assembly, 1893-94, pp. 862-63.

33. The Dispatch, March 3, 1894.

34. _Ibid._, March 4, 1894.

35. The Times, Jan. 7, 8, 1894.

36. McDaniel, op.cit., p. 29.

37. Morton, History of Virginia, pp. 299-300.

38. The World Almanac, 1904, p. 491.

39. McDaniel, op.cit., p. 29.

40. Ibid., p. 30.

41. Ibid., p. 30.

42. Contested Election Case, Yost v. Tucker, 54th Congress, 1st Session, House of Representatives, No. 1636, Vol. 7.

43. Acts of Assembly, 1895-96, p. 763.

44. Pearson v. Board of Supervisors of Brunswick County, et al, 21 S.E.483; 91 Va. 322.

45. Ibid., pp. 485-486.

46. Pearson v. Board of Supervisors..., op.cit., p. 485.

47. This gave Virginia the shortest time limit of all the States.

48. Pearson v. Board of Supervisors..., op.cit., p. 485.

CHAPTER IX

1. Morton, The Negro in Virginia..., p. 134.

2. Morton, History of Virginia, p. 299.

3. Contested Election Cases, Virginia.

4. McDaniel, op.cit., p. 11.

5. The Times, May 11, 1900.

6. Constitution of 1868, Art. IV.

7. The Dispatch, Nov. 7, 1888.

8. Ibid., Nov. 6, 7, 8, 1897.

9. The Times, May 6, 1900.

10. Acts of Assembly, 1899-1900, p. 835.

11. McDaniel, op.cit, p. 12.

12. Acts of Assembly, 1899-1900, pp. 835-36.

13. The Times, May 3, 1900.

14. Ibid.

15. Snavely, op.cit., p. 20.

16. The Times, May 4, 1900, quoting from the Washington Post.

17. Ibid., May 11, 1900.

18. The Dispatch, May 25, 26, 1900; The Times, May 26, 27, 1900.

19. The Dispatch, June 7, 1900.

20. Only 30 out of the 65 white counties favored the convention.

21. United States Census, 1900 and The Dispatch, June 7, 1900.

22. The Dispatch, June 7, 1900.

23. The Times, May 30, 1900.

24. Acts of Assembly, Extra Session, 1901.

25. The local press during the period, June 1900-June 1901.

26. Thomas, A. F., The Virginia Constitutional Convention and its Possibilities, p. 16.

27. Ibid., p. 20.   30. Ibid., pp. 21-22   33. Ibid., p. 23.

28. Ibid., p. 21.   31. Ibid., p. 22.   34. Ibid., p. 25.

29. Ibid., p. 21.   32. Ibid., p. 22   35. Ibid., p. 23.

36. The Times, May 6, 1900.

CHAPTER X

1. The Times, May 6, 8, 1900.

2. The Times, June 11, 1901. The Honorable John Goode, "who had served his State with distinction in the Secession Convention," was elected president.

3. The Dispatch, June 12, 1901. The Republicans were from the Black Belt and the West.

4. Proceedings and Debates of the Virginia Constitutional Convention, 1901-02, Vol. II, p. 2959 (Thom.)

5. Ibid., p. 2966 (Thom)

6. Constitution of 1867-68, Art. III, Sec. 5.

7. Debates, Vol. II, pp. 3-16.

8. Ibid., pp. 17-18.

9. Debates, Vol. II, p. 2964.

10. Ibid., Vol. II, p. 2965. (Thom)

11. Ibid., Vol. II, p. 3070.

12. Ibid.

13. Ibid., p. 3069.

14. Ibid., p. 2979.

15. Ibid., Vol. II, p. 2979.

16. Ibid., p. 3068.

17. Ibid., Vol. II, p. 3063.

18. By an "understanding clause" was meant a provision which would enable the election officials to exclude Negroes, on the ground that they did not "understand" the constitution, and, at the same time, whites could easily be let in.

19. Ibid., p. 2972.

20. Ibid.

21. Ibid.

22. Ibid.

23. Ibid., pp. 2972-73. Reference was probably being made to the case of Williams v. Mississippi in which the Supreme Court upheld clearly disfranchising sections of the Mississippi constitution on the grounds that its "understanding clause" did not actually discriminate against the Negro "on account of race, color or previous condition of servitude," and that "it has not been shown that their actual administration was evil, only that evil was possible under them." This case, 170 U.S. 213, was the first in which the Justices of the United States Supreme Court sanctioned the revision of southern constitutions for the purpose of disfranchising the Negro.

24. Ibid.

25. Ibid.

26. Atlantic Monthly, Vol. 88, Oct. 1901, p. 434.

27. Debates, Vol. II, p. 2973.

28. Ibid.

29. Ibid.

30. Ibid, Vol. II, p. 2974.

31. Ibid

32. Ibid., p. 3076.

33. Ibid.

34. Ibid., pp. 3076-77.

35. Ibid., pp. 3077-78.

36. Constitution of Virginia, 1901-02, Article I, sec. 6.

37. The unprecedented length of this article reflects the determination of the convention to effectively eliminate the Negro vote. The franchise article in Virginia's Constitution of 1867-68 embraced less than two pages and contained only 7 sections and paragraphs, as compared with that in the Constitution of 1901-1902, which covered four and a half pages, 22 separate sections and over 37 paragraphs. The entire Constitution contained 65 pages of printed matter, 8 pages of schedules, and 24 pages of registration ordinances--a classic example of exaggerated and over-codified state constitutions!

38. Article II, Sec. 19.

39. Debates, Vol. II, p. 2993.

40. Ibid., Vol. II, p. 2972

41. Article II, Section 20.

42. Ibid.   43. Ibid.

44. Ibid., Sec. 21.

45. Act. II, Sec. 30.

46. Debates, Vol. II, p. 3076.

47. Acts of Assembly, extra session, 1901, pp. 262-267.

48. The Nation, Vol. 75, Dec. 25, 1902, p. 496.

49. Debates, Vol. II, p. 3254; The Times, May 3, 1901.

50. Acts of Assembly, extra session, 1901, pp. 262, 263, 265.

51. Ibid., p. 267.

52. The Dispatch, April 22, 29, 1900.

53. Debates, Vol. II, pp. 3131, 117-307, 3155.

54. The Dispatch, April 5, 1902.

55. Ibid., April 28, 29, 1902.

56. Fourteen people in one of these "mass meetings" adopted a resolution favoring proclamation. Debates, Vol. II, p. 3155.

57. Ibid., Vol. II, p. 3259.

58. Lobinger, C. S. - The People's Law, p. 414.

59. Oberholtzer, E. P., The Referendum in America, p. 114.

60. Hoar, R. S., Constitutional Conventions, p. 219.

61. Oberholtzer, op.cit., p. 113. (Two years later this action by Mississippi was contested in the case of Sproule v. Fredericks and the court held that the legislature did not have the authority to bind a convention to refer its work to the approval of the people.)

62. Lobinger, op.cit., p. 324.

63. Even the secession ordinance had been submitted to the Va. electorate.

64. Kamper v. Hawkins, 1 Virginia Cases, 20.

65. The Nation, Vol. 75, Dec. 25, 1904, p. 496.

66. Even the majority of the newspapers throughout the State had demanded that the constitution be submitted to the people: The Dispatch, April 6, 1902.

67. Debates, Vol. II, p. 3260.

68. Brenaman, op.cit., p. 93.

69. A Republican from the County of Mecklenbury refused to take the oath. His seat was declared vacant, Feb. 6, 1903. Journal, House of Delegates Sess. 1902-1904.

70. 101 Va. 829; 44 S.E. 754.

71. Ibid., p. 832.

72. The Nation, Vol. 75, Dec. 25, 1902, p. 496.

73. 194 U.S. 147.

74. 194 U.S. 153.

75. 194 U.S. 153.

76. Ibid.

77. 194 U.S. 153.

78. Brickhouse v. Brooks, et al., 165 Federal Reporter 534.

79. This case was brought under Section 1979 of the Revised Statutes of the United States, which forbade any person to deprive another of rights, privileges and immunities guaranteed by the Constitution or laws of the United States.

80. The United States Circuit Court for the Eastern District of Virginia at Norfolk.

81. Brickhouse v. Brooks, et al. 165 Federal Reporter 545.

82. File No. 1762, Clerk of the U. S. District Court, Richmond.

83. McDaniel, op.cit., p. 134.

84. Brickhouse v. Brooks, 165 Federal Reporter 546.

CHAPTER XI

1. The Census of 1900 gave the number of male Negroes in Virginia over 21 as 146,122 and the number of male men above 21 as 301,379.

2. World Almanac, 1910, Virginia, p. 491.

3. Ibid.

4. Journal and Documents of the Va. Constitutional Convention, 1901-02, Documents.

5. Journal, Document VIII, Auditor of Public Accounts.

6. Ibid., Document XVII.

7. The World Almanac, 1910, Virginia, p. 491.

8. At this time two-thirds or more of the Republicans in the state were Negroes.

9. The Nation, Vol. 75, Dec. 25, 1902, p. 496.

10. Ibid., p. 496.

11. The Times-Dispatch, April 1, 1905. The number of white men registered was 276,000.

12. McDaniel, op.cit., p. 48.

13. This, of course, was because the constitution required that, in order to vote, one's poll tax for the past three years must have been paid.

14. Shavely, op.cit., p. 35.

15. Harris, A.L., The Negro as Capitalist, p. 75.

16. Even a superficial examination and comparison of the Republican national platforms of 1896-1912, with those prior to 1880 shows this pronounced move to the right.

17. Interview at Richmond.

18. Interviews at Richmond and with Dr. Abram L. Harris.

19. 234 U.S. 347.

20. 273 U.S. 536, 1926.

21. Texas Revised Civil Statutes, 3093a.

22. Texas Laws, 1927, Chapter 67.

23. 286 U.S. 73.

24. In this 5-4 decision, Justices McReynolds, VanDevanter, Sutherland and Butler dissented.

25. Nixon v. Condon, p. 84.

26. Ibid., p. 85.

27. Ibid., p. 88.

28. Ibid., p. 88.

29. Grovey v. Townsend, 295 U.S. 45.

30. Ibid., p. 50.   31. Ibid., p. 53.

32. Publications of the Michigan Political Science Association, Vol. VI, No. 1, March 1905. This view is borne out in the case of DeWalt v. Bartley, 146 Pa. 543.

33. 33 Fed. (2d) 177.

34. Acts of Assembly, 1920, Sect. 28.

35. Constitution of Virginia, 1901-02, Art. II, Sec. 36.

36. 111 Va. 859.

37. West v. Bliley, p. 179.

38. Ibid., p. 180.   39. Ibid., p. 180.   40. Ibid., p. 180.

41. 42 Fed. (2d) 101.

42. 16 S.E. 85.

43. Ibid., p. 87

44. Communication from the editor of the Richmond News-Leader.

45. Johnson, James Weldon, A Negro Looks at Politics, American Mercury, No.28, 1928, p. 93.

46. Seligman, H. J., The Negro's Influence as a Voter, Current History,1928. No. 28, p. 231.

47. The Washington Daily News, March 24, 1938.

CHAPTER XII

1. It will be remembered that between 1867 and 1884 the Democrats were known as "Conservatives."

2. City Registrar's figures. The total population of the City in 1920 was 117,574 whites and 54,041 colored.

3. On the basis of the number of Negroes 21 years or over.

4. City Registrar's figures.

5. Personal Communication from Mr. E. R. Carter.

6. McDaniel, op.cit., p. 55.

7. The World Almanac, 1922, Virginia, p. 896.

8. _Ibid._   9. _Ibid._

10. The Richmond News Leader, April 20, 1925.

11. _Ibid._ 12. _Ibid._, Nov. 8, 1920.   13. _Ibid._

14. The Washington Daily News, March 24, 1938.

15. _Ibid._ 16. _Ibid._

17. These figures were found by dividing the total votes of these States by the number of Congressmen elected. Mississippi only polled an average of 20,260 votes in electing each of her 8 Congressmen in 1936 and South Carolina only cast an average of 16,490.

18. The Washington Daily News, March 24, 1938.

19. MacCorkle, W.A., _The Negro and the Intelligence and Property Franchise_, p. 23.

20. _Ibid._

21. Acts of Assembly, 1902.

22. _Ibid._, 1912, pp. 330-31. After 12 months from the adoption of this law by a city, no Negro could move into a "white district."

23. _Ibid._, 1926, p. 947.

24. _Ibid._, 1930, p. 97.

25. Harris, _op.cit._, p. 103.

26. The Washington Daily News, March 24, 1938.

27. Davis v. Allen, _op.cit._

28. Lewinson, _op.cit._, p. 117.

29. Gravely, W. H., _Can the Water be Made Fine?_ section on the "Negro Question, p. 28.

30. _Ibid._, p. 28.

31. _Ibid._, p. 33.

32. Personal communication from Mr. E. R. Carter.